God in the Gutter

A memoir of hope from the darkness of child sexual abuse and self-abuse.

To Joanne,
The "best-est" neighbor
a gal can have...
(not a bad deputy either :))
Lotsa Love,
Deborah Silva

Deborah Silva

*This book is dedicated to my sister, Rhonda Guess, who shared
so much of this journey with me and continues to support
and encourage me to this day.*

*It is also dedicated to the many women
and children who have been crushed by abuse.
There is hope and a life for you!*

Contents

1 - All That Glitters

Mojave Desert, 1969

Our ankle-length gowns appropriately shimmered, our tiaras sparkled, and our underarms threatened rebellion against that day's anti-perspirant application. All around us, the mid-morning desert spread gold from east to west and north to south. Sunlight danced around unmoving tumbleweed, stock-still in the absence of even a whispered breeze. The two-lane asphalt ribbon, a melting river in the approaching heat, glimmered empty to the distant horizon in both directions. The left rear tire of my faded metallic-gold Corvair melted flat like candle wax into the abyss of State Route 58 somewhere outside of the town of Boron.

I only know it was outside of Boron because I had just picked up Miss Boron, the reigning beauty queen of that relatively unknown desert burg. We were on our way to smile and wave from the floats in yet another small-town summer parade. The satiny sash draped over my own shoulder read "Miss California City." We both stood, two princesses, a mirage in the middle of a thirsty desert, our high heels digging into the dry grit of sand at the highway's edge, gazing at the flat tire. Our soon-to-be-pasted smiles struggled to find outlet in our current dilemma: stranded in the midst of this vast Mojave wasteland.

In the distance, a disturbance on the glistening horizon emerged. We both saw it at the same time, both hope and

1

apprehension reflecting in each other's gazes. My hand wrapped around the tire iron … just in case … as the approaching unknown and non-descript automobile rolled to a stop behind mine. Nearly half-a-dozen soldiers in short-sleeved tan uniforms, with silly grins plastered all over their faces, spilled from the vehicle like erupting volcanic lava.

"Is there a problem ladies?"

ℭ   ℭ   ℭ   ℭ   ℭ

My less-than-meteoric rise to almost famous, and the journey to that day's parade, began a few weeks earlier, just after my senior year and graduation from Mojave High School, smack dab in the middle of the very desolate Mojave Desert. The only glitch in my step had been failing my first attempt at my driver's test to obtain that coveted California driver's license. I scored nearly perfect the second time around and was thus able to drive my graduation-present Corvair, complete with pending payments, (and repaired flat tire), to the Antelope Valley Fair parade in the not-so-booming metropolis of Lancaster, California.

I had entered the local California City beauty pageant for the fun and glamour, complete with an archrival as the anticipated winner. Besides the intimidating interviews, part of the competition included a fashion show. I had loved runway modeling with the Teen Fashion Board during my junior year of high school in San Jose, so for the California City contest, I strode the pageant's fashion runway with the elegance of an experienced model.

For the final event of the pageant, the five finalists donned evening gowns. My silky white gown shimmered, along with my nerves, while my long brown hair tumbled over my shoulders. Bright sunlight bathed the wooden deck of the

California City recreation center while the audience watched from the troop-like formation of the white deck chairs. The sky glittered brilliant blue, sparkling off the lake surrounding the center. Each girl delivered a few-minute speech about herself and answered that dreaded unknown question. I don't recall my dreaded question, but my speech was well-practiced. Though I didn't expect the crown, I knew I had done well. I wanted to win more than I was willing to admit.

Then it was done. Damp with perspiration and nervously congratulating one another, the contestants waited behind thick glass walls. Giddy smiles hid the hope that each had outperformed her competitors. The judges completed deliberations. The doors opened. The emcee's voice jarred each girl's heart to a stop.

"And ... the fourth runner-up is ..." The disappointed princess, with a contrived smile, stepped out to the deck while each of the rest of us breathed a momentary sigh of relief.

He announced the third runner-up ... and the second runner-up. Tensions mounted. My archrival and I, still behind the glass walls, avoided each other's eyes. The emcee babbled on about inconsequential matters, stalling. We held our breath.

"And the first runner-up is ..." He announced the other girl's name.

My mother squealed from the audience. "She did it!"

I basked in the acclaim as they pinned the tiara to my hair, draped the sash over my shoulder, and placed the roses in my arms. I savored the moment. An insatiable need inside me could no longer settle for second-best. I had become an approval junkie.

The Miss California City title opened many doors for me. The city manager offered me a public relations job which I gladly accepted, eager to push aside and forget my existing job as a hotel maid. That summer of 1969 filled with fairs, parades, and carnival rides with Senators. I rode the rock-o-plane with Senator Barry Goldwater Jr. There were bigger pageants with famous entertainers and choreographed performances throughout Southern California. My opportunities for dating increased exponentially. I devoured the attention. My long-time boyfriend Ted was quickly fading into the past as a helicopter door-gunner half a world away in the Viet Nam War.

So many possibilities loomed on my horizon. I had graduated in the top-ten of my class. I had been accepted to a prominent fashion school in Los Angeles. As Miss California City, my public relations job transferred to the Hollywood corporate offices for Great Western Cities, the financial investment company responsible for the very existence of California City. The Director of Marketing, a senior-level middle-aged boys-club buddy, defined my job description in Hollywood as, "Just look pretty." I knew my dreams of a whirlwind career in the exciting world of fashion were very much attainable. Fame and fortune awaited me ... the darkness of my childhood would be forever buried.

ଔ   ଔ   ଔ   ଔ   ଔ

A few short months later, in the middle of a fitful sleep, a spasm jerked my body awake. For a brief moment my head rose off the pillow, a whimper pushed past my throat. It took me a couple of minutes to realize where I was. Gradually my eyes adjusted, and I recognized the shadowy outlines of my own bedroom in North Hollywood. A dim glow from a nearby streetlight filtered through the Venetian blinds, just enough for me to make out some of the forms in my room. The other empty bed reminded me that my roommate, Kathy, was away for the weekend. I heaved a great sigh, laid back on my pillow and gazed blankly towards the ceiling.

I had shared dinner earlier that evening with Dennis, the lead singer from the band at the fraternity party Kathy and I attended the previous week. That previous week, I had been, well … intoxicated … just like everyone else at the party. Wanton behavior emerged when I drank, and Dennis' raw, sensual performance triggered desire in me. Dennis expected that wanton behavior tonight, but I wasn't drinking with dinner. Without the dull edge of alcohol, I tired of him by the time we ordered dessert. I drove home in my own car, dragged myself up the stairs to my second-floor apartment and collapsed, still dressed, in a heap on my bed.

Vacant thoughts lulled my mind. I hated the person I had become.

Ted, why did you have to leave? I cursed the government that stole him from me; the government that sent him to that execrable Viet Nam war.

For two years, Ted had been the focal point in my life. When he was there, things made sense. I had only been in North Hollywood a few months and had already forgotten the names of most of the men I partied with. Despite my status as Miss California City, I needed constant approval, someone to value me. I had the looks and body to attract any man I wanted. It was easy to find affirmation in a man's arms, but physical lust offers only temporary relief, a counterfeit relief for desired love.

Kathy worked as a hostess at a popular restaurant. She constantly met guys who had a friend who wanted to go out with her friend. I was happy to oblige. There were weekends in Palm Springs, dinners in Santa Barbara, and endless parties at the singles' apartment complexes. Kathy and I left our restrictive dorms at the fashion school and rented our own apartment.

Barely eighteen, we figured we knew all we needed to know to make our own decisions and choose our own behavior.

Lessons came fast and I succumbed with ignorant fervor. When I was modeling, photographers were always interested in more than just taking my pictures. I dated struggling actors who were usually rude and self-centered and could not be trusted. Successful actors were arrogant, "Wannabees" revolting. Everyone I met clung to some fringe of show business. For anything anyone desired, there were willing participants, willing guides, and eager masters. In Hollywood, it wasn't hard to touch the seedy side of life. It reached to consume any who stepped in its path. I knew I was sinking into depravity but didn't know what to do about it. It nearly cost me my life.

Kathy set me up with Walt, a motorcycle racer, fifteen years older than me. His rugged coarseness, along with a lustful sense of his desire for me, attracted me. He made me his showcase at the racetrack and pulled strings for me to be one of the "Trophy Girls." It was with Walt that I first smoked marijuana.

Once again, I quickly tired of the superficial love and therefore tired of Walt. He had been repairing my Corvair, so I had to pick up my car before officially ending the relationship. But I was naïve. I should have waited till I was safely in my car, ready to drive off, before letting him know it was over. I thought I was being sensitive and kind to kiss him goodbye.

Walt refused to return my kiss. He stood in silence, his tall, husky frame towering over me. A cold glare oozed from his alcohol-reddened eyes. A muscle at the corner of his mouth began to twitch. The smell of him overwhelmed me. I realized I never did like the stench of beer and cigarettes.

"Where are my keys?" I pulled away from him.

He remained rooted and silent, his eyes burning holes through me.

"My keys," I challenged, gesturing with an open hand.

"I'll get your car," he clipped, with his back already towards me. "I still need to put some oil in it." The door slammed behind him.

I waited on the frayed plaid sofa. The dark apartment, with shades always drawn, reeked of his cigarettes. I wondered what I had found so appealing about him in the first place.

It was taking an awfully long time for him to get my car and I grew impatient. I walked outside just in time to see him skid to a stop with one wheel upon the sidewalk. He burst out of the car, flung my keys to the ground by my feet, and then stormed into his apartment without a word. I slid onto the driver's seat, glanced at my mirrors, maneuvered the car off the sidewalk, and sped away. That was the last of Walt, or so I thought.

Driving on the 405 north, over the hills, away from Walt, I began to lose track of my surroundings. A sudden truck horn startled me. Adrenaline kicked in when the lights of the truck loomed large in my rear-view mirror. For a moment, I couldn't remember where I was or even where I had been driving. Frightened, I pulled off to the side of the road. *Did I fall asleep while driving?*

Sitting alone on the side of a Los Angeles freeway at night was a dangerous place for a single female. There had been recent news stories of disappearances, rapes, and death. I flashed on my emergency blinkers. My consciousness wavered but I snapped awake and rolled down my window. Cool air rushed over my face. I couldn't get enough of it. I stuck my head out the window.

I wish a highway patrolman would drive by. I have to get home ... what is wrong with me?

I pulled slowly out into the lane, blinkers still flashing. It took all my energy to focus, to make myself pay attention to the road in front of me.

Where is a highway patrolman?

Cars whizzed past. Some honked. I needed all my concentration to keep moving forward. Heaviness flowed through my veins, weighing down my arms. My hips, like lead, pushed into the seat. I fought to maintain consciousness.

I have to stay awake. I have to make it to North Hollywood.

Flash. Flash. Flash. My emergency blinkers reflected off my rear-view mirror like a distant strobe light.

Where is a highway patrolman? I don't think I can make it. What is wrong with me?

Finally, the lights of the 101 loomed ahead of me, like a time-lapsed photograph, streams of color speeding through the darkness. I eased around the off ramp, counting each post of the guardrails. My head rested on the door of my car. I gulped cool air. I struggled to focus on the pavement. Then I saw the hospital.

Gasping for breath and nearly losing consciousness, I stumbled into the emergency room. A disheveled, pudgy, middle-aged nurse grabbed my arms and jostled me to a gurney.

"Drugs, these kids and their drugs," she mumbled. She didn't bother to close the curtain, nor did she make sure I was warm enough, cool enough, or needed water or anything.

"I haven't taken any drugs," I sputtered.

"Spend a night in jail instead of a comfortable hospital, that'll straighten you up a bit." She walked away grumbling to anyone who would listen. "Kids today, they think they're 'all that'. What they need is a good whoopin'. That'll set 'em straight." She sank behind a counter and directed a younger nurse to telephone the police.

I tried to reposition my arms laying limp on the gurney, but they didn't respond. The younger nurse who telephoned the police stood at my side, her voice gentle and caring. "Is there somebody I can call for you?" Tears spilled from my eyes.

I recited my parents' phone number. They lived two hours away. I must have lost consciousness because the next thing I saw was my stepfather talking to the police.

Walt had the last word. The exhaust pipe on my Corvair was stuffed with rags. The carbon monoxide poisoning nearly took my life.

ଓ   ଓ   ଓ   ଓ   ଓ

Depravity? Yes, I was on that road. My mind returned to the darkened bedroom around me. I drifted off to sleep but peace did not settle in. Again, I became aware of the filtered light through my bedroom window. Something caught my attention to my left, something through my bedroom door.

Three dark, hooded figures drifted into my room from the dark hallway. The forms appeared human, but they were not walking, they floated just above the floor. The tallest figure stretched out his arms, large sleeves drooping. He beckoned me towards him. My body rose up off the bed. Something pulled me towards the apparition. Terror rose in my throat, but my silent screams were heard by no one. Again, I tried to scream. Again, my throat tightened, but no sounds came out.

"NO," I finally blurted. A muffled gurgle, but it was sound. My ears heard it. The three figures disappeared.

I lay shaking on my sweat-soaked bed. How had it come to this? How had I fallen so quickly from a sparkling tiara to the dark and terrifying nightmare I now lived?

ଔ   ଔ   ଔ   ଔ   ଔ

2 – Daddy Doesn't Live Here Anymore

"Every girl pretends she is a princess at one point, no matter how little her life is like that."
Alex Flinn

Redwood City, CA, 1958

I kicked it! Stomped it! Crushed it! Hissed in triumph!

Well, I wanted to kick it, stomp it, and crush it. But I was never brave enough to act out the imaginations of my mind. My inner wild child never ventured outside my straitjacket of insecurity, but rather huddled like a scream from a waking nightmare heard only as a crushed whisper. Instead, I nudged the toe of my worn saddle shoe against the dirty red paint peeling from the concrete curb outside my second-grade classroom. The paint curls shattered and disappeared into the surrounding grit of the sidewalk.

Voices swelled behind me, then disappeared without inviting me. Tears threatened, but I blinked them back. Another curling paint finger crumbled under my destructive saddle shoe. The school bus rumbled and shuddered to a stop just past my errant toes. Blowing dust swirled upwards like ragged little whirlwinds as the tires grabbed at the gritty little victims of my crime, now crushed in the gutter under the weight of the aging rubber. Black, stinky exhaust fumes burned my nostrils. A lump of dread welled in my throat. I did not want to go home.

The bus coughed and sputtered. A handful of noisy boys pushed past me, shoving each other, fighting to be first through the open bus door. School let out early that day. Mom would soon be expecting me to walk through the front door of our house on Meadow Lane. I willed the world to stop, but everything still moved. Emptiness waited at Meadow Lane.

I stepped back away from the bus—just one step—then stopped. I didn't want anyone to notice me backing away. I pretended to study my feet for a moment, then looked up again. Messy brown curls fell from my eyes. I squinted against the sun, peering intently at the sprawling pink-stucco two-story building down the street from the schoolyard. The sign said Villa Rosa Apartments. To me it was a fairytale castle. A forbidden castle. I imagined myself wandering its grand hallways.

I took another step. My shoe caught in a crack in the concrete. I stumbled, then regained my balance. My face burned with embarrassment. I inched further away from the yawning mouth of the monstrous yellow bus. I pushed the house on Meadow Lane out of my mind. It was lunchtime and Daddy lived in the Villa Rosa Apartments. I turned and scurried towards the crosswalk.

Daddy made wonderful grilled cheese sandwiches. I picked up my pace as I imagined the crispy buttery bread. I could almost taste the stretchy melted cheese. Visions danced in my mind of the golden sandwich lifted warm from the heavy black skillet. Daddy would cut it with a pancake turner, corner to corner, making two triangles on my plate. I broke into a run.

I arrived at the pink castle panting, gasping for breath. I stopped, stood tall, pulled back my shoulders, and sucked in my breath. I stood for just a moment at the bottom of the stairs, waiting for my heart to stop pounding. Grasping the wrought iron handrail, I pulled myself up, one step at a time. His doorway loomed in front of me like the gated entrance to a forbidden land, my pink wonderland. I knocked on the door. Butterflies danced in my stomach. I heard his footsteps and shifted from one impatient foot to the other. The door opened.

"Debbie Jo," Daddy stammered. "What ... what are you doing here?"

I grinned, blissfully unaware of the dilemma he now faced.

He sighed, fixed his eyes on me, and pursed his lips. "Hey Sweetie, come on in." He squatted, gathered me up in his arms, and plopped me down inside the darkened apartment, not a castle at all. Bits of sunlight danced on the worn hardwood floor wherever it forced its way through a crack in the closed Venetian blinds.

"How about sharing some lunch with your ol' dad?"

Well, that's exactly what I came here to do.

Sitting at the small table in his cramped kitchen, I savored the grilled cheese sandwich. I studied the cracked corner of the yellow Formica tabletop, memorizing every dark yellow vein within the borders of the tarnished chrome frame. A table with veins of gold and silver trim. I rocked back and forth on the yellow vinyl-upholstered chair, my princess throne. The four chrome legs staunchly clung to the floor preventing the chair itself from actually rocking. Daddy didn't talk much, but I reveled in his company.

I grasped for any memory I could capture in my mind, clinging to my fairy-tale castle. I imagined my dad a king and I was his princess. Kings were aloof. They were busy. They had important things to do. They didn't have time to play with their princesses, just like my Daddy. But a king's princess was a very important little girl. Everyone in the kingdom knew who she was. Her maidens told her she was beautiful. She wore fine clothes and ate fancy food. All the children wanted to play with the princess. She was never alone. There was always someone to hug her. Someone to love her.

But lunch was over much too soon. Daddy had to go back to work. He drove me home, without once looking at me. His long, bony hands gripped the top of the steering wheel. Silence filled the car until it rolled to a stop at 17 Meadow Lane. Tears burned my eyes when Daddy opened the door on my side of the old 1946 Chevrolet. I scooted towards him and looked up, hoping he might change his mind. But the sun was behind his head. I couldn't see his face. He just stood, waiting. My ruffled skirt slid up and my leg scraped and stuck for a moment on the vinyl trim of the seat. I stumbled to the driveway below. With my leg stinging, I shuffled behind Daddy, up the worn, pink, cement walkway towards the dark-green, front door of our house.

The door burst open and Mommy stomped out onto the porch. She glared at Daddy. Her lips squeezed tight. She didn't even look at me. Then her words spit out like an angry river pounding any rocks in its path. I skittered past her legs and curled up against the wall of the entry hall. I escaped to a place inside my head where it was quiet. Time stood still in that place. I could wander and explore, leaving the world behind me. A princess in her palace gardens. When I dared to mentally venture back into the room, Daddy was gone.

Although Daddy had only moved out a few months earlier, I couldn't remember what it was like to have him in our house. In my mind, I can see every room, but I can't find Daddy in any of them. I don't know where he is. The rooms are empty.

They are quiet. Paper-doll princesses lie scattered on the floor. There is no laughing in the house on Meadow Lane.

I can't remember him anywhere. Not even when I peeked around the heavy, green curtain from the stage at my dance recital. The room was filled with mommies and daddies, grandmas and grandpas, brothers and sisters. But the chair next to Mommy was empty.

There were eight of us little girls, each wearing shiny Mary Jane tap shoes and big-sleeved, black-satin, graduation gown costumes. Miss Martha clapped her hands. Time to line up. The other girls giggled and scurried into place. I wasn't ready. My stomach knotted up. *Daddy's not here yet.*

The "gowns" were cut so short, they barely covered my matching black-satin panties. My flat-board graduation cap kept sliding off my head as I tapped my way onto the stage at the end of the chorus line. It finally fell to the floor. I wanted to hide behind the curtains. Instead, I performed the rest of the recital bareheaded, eyes on the floor. Daddy didn't see. He wasn't in the audience.

Sometimes after school even Mommy wasn't home. On those days, she let me go to Judy and Joani's house, right across the street from our house, where there were hugs and laughing. The warm dining room welcomed its guests with treats and goodies, and a mother's smiles. Judy and Joani's mom made lunch for me. But one time, after a particularly delicious tuna and pickle sandwich, I didn't finish my glass of milk. When Mommy arrived to pick me up, she demanded I drink the rest of it. By then the milk was warm. I gagged with each swallow. It made me so sick, I never drank milk again ... unless, of course, it came in the form of a chocolate milkshake. It wasn't long after that, that Judy and Joani's house burned down.

It happened in the late afternoon, close to the time when all the dads were expected home from work. I was squatting on the sidewalk in front of my house, chalking the first few boxes of a hopscotch game. The smell of cooking dinners filled the air. Autumn warmth lay quiet on the empty street.

Then, without warning, a thunderous explosion slammed the ground. I jolted upright, but my feet gripped the spot where I had been playing.

"Jimmy, what are you ... oooh my God!" Judy and Joani's mother shrieked, then burst out the front door of her house, hugging her purse close to her chest.

At the same time, Judy and Joani's brother, Jimmy, and a couple of his friends, squeezed out a small crack at the side of the slightly-opened garage door. Flames roared out after them, chased them.

"Wha'd you do man?" Jimmy hollered as the boys ran from the exploding inferno.

"I don't know. I don't know," cried the boy with the white-blond hair. They reached the middle of the street. They stumbled and turned towards the angry, fiery fingers now clawing and tearing the roof.

"You idiot!" The dark-haired boy pushed both greasy hands through his hair. "You idiot! You stupid idiot!" He cried and yelled at the same time. He shoved the white-haired boy next to him. "You spilled the gas by the water heater, man!"

"Oh man, oh man, oh man ..." Jimmy slumped to the ground, rocked back and forth, holding his head in his hands. When he looked up, white eyes bulged out of his blackened face.

In just a few heartbeats, the whining sirens of the fire trucks turned into the rumbling of engines powering their massive hoses. The raging fire swallowed the front of the house. Balls of black smoke exploded, blanketing the sky. Grey floating ashes, like snowflakes, drifted across the street, landing on my hair and my hopscotch game. The house burned completely to the ground. The hungry flames left only a few smoldering reminders of charred two-by-four framing—that had once been Judy and Joani's house.

I stood frozen to the sidewalk. The air reeked of wet ashes. The fire engines still rumbled. Firemen in heavy boots shed their jackets and lifted their heavy hoses, rolling them up into the big red trucks. Nobody even noticed me standing there. Alone. I stared, too afraid to move, with only the first few boxes of my hopscotch game.

Where was Daddy in those memories? No matter how hard I try, I can't find him. He didn't come to my rescue during the fire. I couldn't find him when I needed hugs and comfort. He didn't come to my rescue when things happened I couldn't understand. Where was he when my cousin Buddy took me into the bedroom that Sunday afternoon, when all the relatives were visiting? I was only six years old.

Buddy wasn't very tall for his age but what he lacked in height he more than made up for in attitude. Even at eleven years old, he carried a pack of cigarettes in the rolled-up sleeve of his tight, white tee-shirt. His soft blue eyes, shrouded by a lock of brown hair, disguised the menace behind them. Black motorcycle boots peeked out from under grubby low-slung jeans, well-worn from his many dirt bike misadventures.

His dad, my Uncle Earl, usually laughed at Buddy's motorcycle horror stories, often telling them himself. Aunt Betty, always elegantly dressed, and always dangling a cigarette between the first two fingers of her right hand, didn't seem any more concerned about Buddy's activities than his father. None of the aunts or uncles questioned his behavior either, so he pretty much did what he wanted.

Retreating from the heavy mid-day dinner that Sunday, the parents sent all the cousins outside to play while they moved into the living room to chat about "grown-up matters that don't involve children." The younger kids all ran to the swing-set in the grassy back yard. Buddy waited for me at the back door.

"Wait," he said. He peered at me from under his floppy hair, one side of his mouth curved up in a crooked smile. "Let's go hide."

I giggled. We snuck back down the hallway. I worried about getting caught since Uncle Earl said we were all supposed to go outside. But hide-n-seek with Buddy sounded more fun than getting stuck with all the little kids. I felt so grown up at his invitation. We slipped into my little brother's bedroom. Buddy quietly closed the door behind us. Then he unzipped his jeans.

The parents didn't want the kids bothering them, so no one even noticed my swollen red eyes or my quiet tears when I left the room. For a moment, I lingered in the hallway, hoping someone might see me. But no one was paying any attention.

Just a small child who cousin Buddy brought into the bedroom.

છ્ર છ્ર છ્ર છ્ર છ્ર

3 – Alone

*"To feel that you aren't important to your mother leaves a hole.
Most often it is felt as a hole in the heart. It's the hole where
Mother was supposed to be."*
Jasmin Lee Cori

Although my mind is filled with memories of my mom
in our house on Meadow Lane, I never see her face in those
memories. I never felt her sitting next to me, or the soft warmth
of her lap. After I started school, she often had my favorite snack
waiting for me when I got home: a cold hot dog and a carrot. But
she never sat down and shared it with me. She never asked me
how I was or how my day went. Other mothers hugged and
kissed their little girls, but I don't think my mom knew how.

Looking back now, I realize she was the baby of her
family. Her mother named her Joan, pronounced "jo-ann," but
she didn't give her a middle name. Her five brothers and sisters
were already grown up when she was born, so she grew up like
an only child: Joan, no middle name, alone, without brothers
and sisters to play with. Perhaps her mom was too old and tired
by then to consider a middle name, too old and tired to hug and
kiss her. Perhaps she never learned how to hug and kiss. My
mother did give me a middle name: Joan. Oddly though, I
wonder why mine is pronounced simply "Joan," a single syllable.

She did keep a "baby book" of me when I was very little. When I learned to read, she let me read the things she wrote in the book:

"Debbie Jo fell down the stairs today. There was blood everywhere…"

"Debbie Jo stepped on the heater vents today. I took her to the doctor and she has second-degree burns on her feet…"

She also had photographs of us at Mt. Lassen and Santa's Village. But I don't remember any of it. It happened before we moved to the house on Meadow Lane, before my brother and sister were born.

I was almost three years old when my sister Rhonda entered my world, a chubby blond bundle of energy whom Daddy affectionately called "Butterball." Less than a year later, my brother Richie was born. As soon as they both could toddle, they bounced, romped, and made blanket tents together. Even when they were sick, they darted everywhere. Mommy was always chasing after them. I had to play by myself. There were no more entries in my baby book.

But there was a moment, a single moment, I remember her by my side. I was four-and-a-half years old.

I awoke from a deep sleep. Soft murmurs rose like a fog all around me. Somewhere in the distance, a child cried.

"I want ice cream," another small voice whimpered nearby.

My eyelids stuck to my eyes, but I finally forced them open. I stared at a dark ceiling from inside a big white crib. I reached over and touched the cold, white bars. Bits of light trickled in from a nearby open door. There were lots of big white cribs in the dimly lit room, like cages, each containing its own waking, frightened child. Pain stabbed my throat.

Someone gently touched my shoulder. "Do you want some Jell-O?" A woman in a white dress and cap. A nurse.

My throat hurt too much to talk. She pushed the little cup of red Jell-O through the bars and set it on the mattress next to my pillow. A dinky white napkin and a small, flat, wooden spoon followed. Then she moved to the next crib.

"Where is Mommy?" I whispered, but nobody answered. I remembered I was in the hospital. They cut out my tonsils and adenoids. Fear wrapped its arms around me, its grip crushing my breath.

Where is Mommy? I was alone in my cage. My eyes began to burn so I squeezed them shut and escaped into the darkness of sleep.

The next thing I remember, I woke up in my own bedroom, in my own bed. Blood soaked my pillow. It was everywhere—on my face and in my hair. I sputtered and tried to get up. Mommy shushed me with a finger to her lips. She wiped my face with a towel then pressed another towel alongside my mouth and nose as Daddy lifted me and carried me to the car.

I was back in the hospital. Doctors and nurses bustled around me until everything went dark.

When I woke up again, sunlight streamed through the high narrow windows of another hospital room. Mommy sat in a chair next to my bed, reading. Strings spilled out of my nose and mouth. Panic edged in and I tried to sit up.

"Don't try to talk." She set her book on the bedside table and eased me back to my pillow.

"It's okay. They're tying packs in behind your nose, on the adenoid bed, like a Band-Aid. There's a feeding tube in your leg." She pointed and I followed her gaze. My left leg wrapped in white gauze and a tube emerged through the bandages at my ankle. Confusion punched at my thoughts. But I felt important. Mommy was with me.

ભ ભ ભ ભ ભ

My grandparents, Daddy's mom and dad, lived right around the corner from us on Meadow Lane. I loved my Grandpa Max. He held me in his lap. His scruffy whiskers tickled my cheeks.

"You're our first grandchild," he beamed. "You always have your family. And you will always be our first grandchild." Then he would look over at my Grandma. His eyes softened and his lips parted, lost in in a memory. "See how pretty she is. See how her blue eyes twinkle." Then he'd look back and wink at me. "You have hazel eyes just like your grandpa."

I smiled and snuggled deeper into his arms, happy my eyes were hazel.

Grandpa's family was Jewish and most of them escaped from Kaiser Wilhelm II's Germany just before Hitler rose to power. He liked to teach me German words. When I sneezed, he always said, "Gesundheit!" Then he informed me the proper response was, "Es besser wie krankeit," (the "w" pronounced like a "v"). "Gesundheit means good health," he explained. "And you reply … 'It's better than sickness.'"

Grandpa often made me laugh. He pretended to act mad and then tease people. He'd usually wink, then exclaim, "I'm so mad I could eat ham!" Grandma told me Jewish people weren't supposed to eat ham.

My grandma was Catholic, and her family disowned her when she married my Grandpa. So, I never met any of Grandma's family. We often had Christmas dinner at Grandma and Grandpa's house and Grandma usually made leg of lamb.

Mommy didn't like lamb, but I looked forward to it every Christmas. I also looked forward to visiting Grandma and Grandpa whenever I could. They wrapped me in warm hugs. They also had a chest freezer on their patio where grandkids could always find popsicles.

Wherever grandkids played, Grandpa held a movie camera, recording the moments. When he pointed it at me, I smiled, I danced, I waved my arms.

"Look at me!"

When the film was full, Grandpa unrolled and set up the movie screen. He threaded the developed film through the projector and click, click, click. The grainy scenes unfolded before our eyes. And there I was, smiling, dancing, waving my arms—looking straight at the camera.

"Look at me!" *See me!*

While I was just six years old, my movie stopped. Daddy didn't live with us anymore. Like a film strip that breaks, the reel spun without purpose, the pictures stopped moving. Life moved in slow motion while the rest of the world passed me by. Stranded. Alone. Frozen in the grainy memory on the screen.

"Look at me!"

After that, Mommy didn't let me go to Grandma and Grandpa's whenever I wanted. She spent a lot of time on the phone, talking to other people. She didn't have time to talk to me. Rhonda and Richie were always off somewhere playing together. I spent a lot of time by myself up in the tree in front of our house. I could climb higher than any of the neighborhood boys. I hid in its leafy branches, losing myself in the pages of a book.

Sunday mornings, Daddy would pick us up and take us to Sunday School. I proudly rode in the front seat of the car with Daddy. Richie and Rhonda squirmed and giggled in the back.

We drove past the Pep Boys auto parts store on the corner with the smiling faces of Manny, Moe, and Jack, and on up the hill to Grace Bible Church. Mom used to sing in the choir at church, but she stopped coming with us when Daddy moved out.

I didn't feel so alone at Sunday school. I journeyed through stories with heroes like Daniel in the lion's den, and David killing a giant with a sling shot. There were pictures of Jesus with little children gathered around him. Everyone smiled in those pictures. Jesus loved the little children. Daddy told me Jesus loved me. But Daddy always dropped me off at home afterwards. Jesus stayed at church.

One evening, Daddy took me to the Cow Palace in San Francisco to see a man named Billy Graham. The monstrous building loomed large in the middle of acres and acres of parking lots filled with cars. I never saw any cows there, so I wondered why they called it a cow palace. Or even a palace, for that matter. It looked like a giant barn big enough to hold entire herds of cattle. When we left the safety of our car, I grabbed Daddy's hand, scurrying to keep up with him amidst the swirling crowds of people. I didn't let go of him until we found our seats. Even then, I scrunched as close as possible to him.

I peered at the distant stage. It looked small from our high-up seats in the cavernous building. The thundering roar of thousands of voices stilled to a whisper when Mr. Graham walked out and stepped up to the pulpit. I leaned forward, straining to hear. Then his voice echoed, reaching to the rows of seats behind us, even the highest rows. He told us all that God loved us and gave his son, Jesus, to die for our sins. I had heard about these things in Sunday school. I had even memorized the verse Mr. Graham quoted from John 3:16:

"For God so loved the world, that he gave his only begotten son, that whosoever believeth in Him shall not perish but have everlasting life." (KJV)

But that night, he spoke directly to me. He looked right at me. He told me Jesus loved ME! It wasn't just a story in a storybook. Jesus was real. And Jesus wanted to live in my heart. Mr. Graham said Jesus was light and would push darkness away. He invited everyone who wanted Jesus to live in their hearts, to come forward and talk to somebody by the stage.

Convinced, I wanted to run forward crying out, "Yes. Yes. Take me. I want Jesus to love me." But crowds of big people streamed down the steps towards the stage. I froze, panic-stricken. My feet wouldn't move.

"Daddy, will you go with me?" I pleaded, pulling on his hand.

"I can't go with you. This is a decision you have to make all by yourself."

Frightened, but determined, I looked once again at the swelling crowds moving forward. Then, for a few moments, I stood alone with the almighty, all-powerful God. The world disappeared from around me, a little six-year-old girl, all alone, but precious to God. I reached out to take the love He offered, took a deep breath, and stepped out into the swirling sea of people.

I touched God that night. But the next day, life did not change. I had questions, but no one answered them. My mom still did not attend church. I still didn't get to spend much time with Daddy. Nobody taught me what I was supposed to do with Jesus in my heart. I already knew one bedtime prayer: "Now I lay me down to sleep. I pray the Lord my soul to keep. And if I die before I wake, I pray the Lord my soul to take." But that prayer only made me worry about dying in my sleep. The life-changing evening at the Cow Palace, and Jesus, faded into a memory of the past.

Like my dad, Jesus, my King, lived in an imagined distant country. His castle was in heaven and I couldn't visit. Though I was his princess, I was still alone, crying in the dark. There was no one to push the lonely darkness away. I tore up all my paper princess dolls and stuffed them in the trash.

Big sister Debbie with toddler pair of Rhonda and Richie.

ൟ ൟ ൟ ൟ ൟ

4 – Tossed by the Waves

*"The most terrible poverty is loneliness and
the feeling of being unloved."*
Mother Theresa

The morning of my seventh birthday, loneliness swamped me like a branch caught upright in a flowing stream. The water continued swirling by. Mom celebrated with what she said was my birthday party, but none of my friends were invited. My aunts and uncles were there, but they just sat around and talked with each other. Nobody brought presents. Except Daddy. He walked in and handed me a tall, skinny, wrapped present, as tall as me. I ripped off the paper and squealed at the shiny, silver pogo stick. I put one foot on the foot peg, eager to try it out. But Mom stopped me.

"I have an announcement," she stated, then waited until all eyes were on her. She fidgeted with her collar and cleared her throat. "The children and I are moving to Colorado."

My stomach knotted. My throat closed.

Daddy didn't say anything. He left.

I needed Grandpa Max. I longed for his lap, his arms wrapped around me, his scruffy face rubbing against mine. Grandpa Max would not be in Colorado.

The aunts and uncles all wished her well. They smiled, chatted about Colorado, and ate more cake.

I jumped on my pogo stick ... and jumped and jumped and jumped. I shut out everything else around me. If I slipped, I stopped, got back on, and jumped some more.

No more grilled cheese sandwiches with Daddy.

Jump. Jump. Jump.

No more hugs from Grandpa.

Jump. Jump. Jump.

Tears burned my eyes. Birthday cake churned in my stomach. Tomorrow was a dark and lonely place. I didn't want to go there.

Against court rulings, Mommy took me, Rhonda, and Richie away from everything we knew. Away from any contact with Daddy. Away from Grandpa Max. A gaping wound opened in my heart.

After days slumped in the car, over endless highways and under dreary gray skies, we arrived at our new house, in our new town: Aurora, Colorado, a suburb of Denver ... a barren neighborhood wrapped in the November chill. I liked the name of our new town. It was the real name of Sleeping Beauty in my large, white, fairytale book—a book I escaped into more often now, dreaming of princes and princesses, fairytales where wishes came true.

But my wishes did not come true.

I trudged to school—alone every day, often through cold, biting snow. I squeezed my books close to my chest, counted the squares in the sidewalk. *Step on a crack, you break your mother's back.* I escaped to the other side of the street from the boys, still snowballs struck my back and my head. I bit back tears. Nobody wanted to be my friend. The girl at the desk next to mine stole my crayons. After school, I hid in my house or in my backyard.

I discovered Mom's Betty Crocker cookbook during that lonely winter. I read the instructions, measured, stirred, cooked, and ate fudge, divinity, and snickerdoodle cookies until I stuffed my face so full, my stomach complained ... or the cookies ran out.

Rhonda and Richie played at nursery school all day. Mom worked in the offices of Sealy Mattress Company—for a few short months. Her boss didn't like her taking time off to tend to sick children or take them to the doctor. Before they fired her, she fell in love with one of the company truck drivers.

Mike was a big man, part American Indian. He stayed at our house most of the time he was in town. He kept a long, coiled leather bullwhip hanging on our utility porch wall. We often snuck peeks at it. When he caught us, he'd grab the whip, uncoil it slowly while staring at us from half-closed eyes, then ... CRACK! His muscled arms threw the whip its full length, slicing the air. It whistled and snapped ... loudly.

"Better obey your mom," he growled. "Or I'll use it on you." Then he winked. The three of us kids liked Mike, but we did not dare cross the line when Mike was there, just in case. We did ask him to crack the whip for us time and time again though.

Around Christmas that year, a fierce blizzard struck Colorado. Mike did not come home from his last truck run. Mom paced the floor all night. I couldn't sleep either, so I tossed and turned on the living-room couch, her infectious worries jabbing me. The wind howled outside, battered our house, and pounded the windows. Just before the morning sun brought refuge to the ravaged night, he finally called. He had fallen asleep while driving and his truck spilled off an icy bridge. It crashed to the snowbank below, coming to rest on its side. Mike's sleeping body survived the impact, cushioned by the pillow of snow and awakened only by the chill on his cheek.

After the accident, Mike didn't come around anymore. He didn't stay at our house. The bullwhip disappeared from the utility room wall. Loneliness moved in again. Mom packed us up and, this time, headed to Nebraska where she had grown up, and where she still had family. Like a scab ripped off before the wound had even healed, Mike disappeared from our lives forever.

Before the winter cold disappeared, we settled into a small house in a crowded row of attached small houses. There were many rows of attached small houses in our neighborhood in Sydney, Nebraska—another desolate, sprawling, flat landscape. We played with other children who lived there, and sometimes we hid with them in their houses when tornadoes threatened. The frequent lightening, thunder, and threat of tornadoes terrified me. I hated Nebraska.

I began suffering frequent problems with diarrhea in Nebraska. "Please, God," I begged as the relentless cramping clenched my body. "Please forgive my sins," I cried. Sitting on the toilet in agony, I drank Pepto Bismol straight from the bottle. At seven years old, I didn't know what wrong things I had done that deserved such punishment, other than hate Nebraska. I just assumed this was evidence of my badness.

I tried so hard to be good, like I thought Jesus wanted— like I thought Mommy wanted. But she never noticed. She just bought more bottles of Pepto Bismol. Maybe Jesus wasn't really in my heart because the punishment continued. Tentacles of self-supposed guilt held me in their grip.

One day, Mommy left without telling us. When we came home from playing with friends, our Aunt Ada met us at the door and told us Mom would be gone for a while. A few days later, we learned Mom was in the hospital and had given birth to a premature baby girl. The baby, Allie, had to stay in the hospital for a whole month before she could come home. When she did come home, she was like a doll that only Mommy could play with. But she didn't have fun playing with her. Mommy was quieter and grumpier than ever. Rhonda, Richie, and I were left to fend for ourselves.

I found out many years later that Mom had taken something to induce the premature delivery. Rather than the desired aborted pregnancy, Allie was born alive.

ભ ભ ભ ભ ભ

With four children now, and a cat, Mom—again—packed us into the 1955 Ford station wagon. We returned to California in time to celebrate my eighth birthday. During our just-under-one-year absence, my dad had moved from Redwood City to Orangevale, in the Sacramento area. He wasn't home when we pulled into the narrow driveway at the little house on Central Avenue. Rhonda, Richie, and I sat on the concrete doorstep … waiting.

When Daddy finally drove up, he wasn't smiling. I jumped up and ran to hug him. But he turned away and walked into the house with Mommy following him. The screen door slammed shut behind them. We were left outside. Rhonda and Richie took off running, laughing, and chasing each other around the outside of the house. Allie still slept in her car bed. I just stood there on the sparse tufts of green grass.

"Daddy? I missed you." But he couldn't hear me now.

When they came out again, Daddy carried a suitcase. Mommy headed to our car and began unloading our boxes. I hurried to Daddy's car. He put his suitcase in the trunk, then looked down at me.

"Now that you're here in California," he said, "You can come visit me." Then he got in his car and drove off. I stood alone at the end of the driveway and watched until his car disappeared over the rise of the two-lane asphalt road.

I visited my father a few times in his new apartment. Instead of grilled cheese sandwiches, we shared jelly and cheese omelets sprinkled with powdered sugar. It is interesting that so many of my memories focus around food. I loved the sweet omelets and would later share them with my own children. As an adult I discovered the same jelly and cheese omelets on the menu of a quaint coffee shop in Carmel. Those omelets fed warm memories of the times spent with my father in Orangevale.

CR CR CR CR CR

Near the end of my third-grade year, Rhonda's kindergarten class took a "field trip" to the first-grade classrooms. One first-grade teacher at school was mean and constantly yelled at the kids. When her high-pitched voice shrieked, kids in her classroom shrunk into bowed heads and hunched shoulders. Kids not in her classroom ran the other direction. After she yelled at Rhonda during that kindergarten field trip, Rhonda decreed at dinner that night, she could not possibly go to Miss Brown's class for first grade. I heartily agreed.

About that same time, Dad announced he was engaged to be married. He scheduled a weekend with his fiancé to take us all to the zoo. Rhonda, Richie, and I waited at the window, each pushing in front of the other to be first to see this new woman in his life. When at last he drove up, we barged out the door. The wooden screen door slammed behind us. When we all piled onto the sidewalk, Daddy opened the car door for our new stepmother-to-be. As she emerged from the darkened car into the bright sunlight of the morning, we all gasped and stood silent. It was Miss Brown!

It was a long and sullen day at the zoo—marked by Miss Brown's constant high-pitched chatter.

A couple weeks later, we came home from school to a babysitter telling us our mother would be gone for a few days. When she finally returned home, it was with our new stepfather. We immediately moved out of Daddy's house and never visited him or his new wife again.

Our stepfather, Gene, whom we were told to call "Dad", was strong and husky, though not tall like Mike had been. Mom told us the story about a group of guys, a little younger than Gene. They were cussing and heckling Gene through the open windows of their Volkswagen van, slowly following Gene while he walked across a parking lot. Finally, Gene turned and stopped directly in front of the van. He stood, arms crossed, feet apart, face glaring with challenge. The van jerked to a stop just inches short of hitting him. Before anyone had a chance to exit the van, Gene reached down and grabbed the underside of the front bumper. He lifted the front of their van up, off the ground, with them in it. When he let it drop, with a violent bounce, the bullies sat silenced. Gene walked off without further harassment.

It wasn't the crack of a bull whip, but it was enough to demand respect. He seemed nice enough, so I was willing to peel back my bandaged aloneness and let him in.

My new dad took me fishing and praised the eight-pound fish I caught. He took me deer hunting and taught me how to use the rifle. I even shot a deer once and he showed me how to track it by the blood. When I brought home a well-rendered still life from my summer school art class, he built an easel for me, purchased some paints, and began teaching me how to use that newfound talent. I thrived in his attention.

It seemed there wasn't anything he couldn't do. A jack-of-all-trades, a master of anything he attempted. He practiced his own veterinary work. Though he had no credentials, his animals survived and thrived. He loved any kind of animal. They loped, and fed, and played in his exquisite paintings and his intricate wood carvings. His woodwork extended to the lathe and planers, filling our home with unique furniture and custom cabinets. He cut and sold firewood, was an expert welder, did all his own auto repairs, and even worked as a rocket-test technician in the aerospace industry. After he and my mom took a class in cake decorating, his cakes were more exquisite than the store-bought cakes from the bakery.

At nine years old, my image of family was inflated like a large and wonderful balloon. Once again, I had a mom and a dad. We lived in the "pink house," a low, sprawling, pink stucco rambler in an eclectic neighborhood filled with bushes, trees, and neighbors who knew each other. We played, ate, and watched television together as a family. When Mom and Dad worked, we came home to our babysitter, an amiable, competent high school senior who lived across the street from us.

The large and wonderful balloon grew bigger and brighter when Mom came home one day wearing a maternity smock. I held my balloon high, gripped it tightly, flourished in its buoyancy. I carried it from home, to school, and back again.

Big, bright balloons herald momentary celebrations. During or after the celebration, some balloons burst suddenly, others lose their air slowly. In my case, the air escaped in unheard whispers until the shock of its emptiness confronted me. Bit by bit, the illusion of happy, family, and security dissipated. I didn't see it happening—because I didn't want to see it. I wanted to be held and loved, to thrive as a "somebody." I held fast to my version of truth. But that truth was a lie. The balloon crumpled limp at my feet.

He praised the eight-pound fish I caught.

ભ ભ ભ ભ ભ

5 - Rude Awakenings

"Childhood should be carefree, playing in the sun; not living a nightmare in the darkness of the soul."
Dave Pelzer

My big white fairytale book of dreams-that-come-true disappeared. In its place, the empty balloon taunted me. As time put on a jacket of familiarity, infatuation with my new dad evolved to anxiety. Trapped in a Stevenson novella, "The Strange Case of Dr. Jekyll and Mr. Hyde," I escaped to the shadows when "Dad" came home from work each evening or emerged from his bedroom in the morning.

At first glance, he offered pleasant greetings like the personable Dr. Jekyll. But then, at an A-minus on my report card, Mr. Hyde pierced me with his deep disappointment at my failure. I could not achieve the pinnacle of his expectations, but, like a carrot dangled, I constantly leapt to grab it, always falling short. He snared me with accolades one moment, then crushed me in my infractions the next. Failure bore down upon me like a heavy anvil. To this day, a rise of nausea confronts me when I think of him as Dad. So please forgive me if I continue to use his given name as I tell this story. I may once in a while say Dad, but only as I am remembering that moment and the term that was used.

The many layers of Gene peeled back, layer, by layer, by layer. In the harsh light of reality, a perverse and rough man emerged from the hero I first worshipped. He looked for reasons to discipline. If there were none, he created one. With no confessor to the presumed crime, he punished us all.

Spankings became a regular event, usually with the "fanny paddle" or, even at one time, a boat oar. Gene grabbed his chosen offender, forced my brother, sisters, or me, to bend over with pants pulled down. The "un-chosen" cowered from shadows. We watched him, his arms held high, like a baseball player swinging a bat, or a golfer, his club. He swung hard, eyes gleaming, with the rush of the game. A contorted dance ensued while he gripped the arm of the writhing, screaming child who pulled and twisted in a futile attempt to escape the torture. From the shadows, or sometimes from the other side of a closed door, we winced at the sound, felt the pain, as if it was happening to us. Mom held her hands to her face, her lips pressed tight, but she did not interfere.

We had no advocate. Didn't realize we needed one. We belonged to him now. I learned years later that he, along with my mom, had made threats until my father released his children into adoption. Through a bureaucratic swipe of the pen, the name on my birth certificate changed to Gene's last name: Hauser … my biological father's name erased from my history.

Mom walked under the weight of his shadow, apparently content bearing the burden of his pedestal. I grasped relentlessly for tidbits of his approval, nuggets he handed out with chains of expectations attached. I endured the inflicted pain as evidence of my badness.

Gene brought his own motherless daughter into the family after my third sister, Linnie, was born. Renee had been raised by doting grandparents who felt sorry for the child whose mother died in childbirth. Gene still blamed the doctors, but he poured out his misplaced anger on the now-sullied child. She showed no bonds of affection towards her previously absent father. She came with her pony, her toys, and her attitude. We considered Renee an intruder, a spoiled brat, and saw no reason to gain her affection.

Our stepsister's poor grades in school always gave Gene an opportunity for beating another bare bottom. Her screams shrieked from behind closed bedroom doors as the crack of the paddle snapped over and over like the tattoo of slow-motion artillery, on, and on, and on. Lumps of dread mingled with sympathy in our chests, even for Renee. Our minds begged it to end, but we kept our mouths shut. We were grateful we were good students.

My stepfather also investigated thoroughly any small injury in any of us girls. Being the oldest, this "investigation" happened more often to me than the beatings. Bearing a façade of deep concern over the most minute of injuries, his hands examined my body in areas that did not even relate to the trauma. His fingers probed into very inappropriate private parts, touching, exploring, questioning. "Does it hurt here? Does it hurt here?" I hated that part of him.

Often in the middle of the night, Gene left the privacy of his bedroom and wandered the house completely naked. He stopped at my open bedroom door, the door he required stay open at night. His eyes pierced the darkness, his gaze locked on me. Nausea bubbled in my throat and I pulled the covers tight, turning my head away, pretending sleep.

In the daytime, I grabbed at distractions like school, camping trips, and my friend Leila's Finnish family with their authentic Finnish sauna, their hand-dug swimming pool, and happy family breakfasts of oatmeal and ice cream. Like a pasted smile for a momentary pose, I still held tight to my picture of family ... with me in it.

 CR CR CR CR CR

The early sixties rolled in to the sounds of the Civil Rights Movement, The Flintstones, and Nikita Khrushchev pounding his shoe on a table at the United Nations. Adults still gossiped about Elvis Presley gyrating on the Ed Sullivan Show and Hawaii had just become a state.

We moved into one of the new ticky-tacky housing tracts, popular at that time. Block after block of three or four similar floorplans painted different colors or facing different directions. The spacious green yards offset the conceptual suggestion of cookie cutter abodes.

At school in fourth grade, life was good. I was part of the "in-crowd" at Palisades Elementary School. There were six of us in this very elite group, three girls and three boys. We often passed notes back and forth in class that read: "I love you. Do you love me?" Then there were the appropriate yes or no boxes to be checked. Although we all associated with other kids on a limited basis, we were the ones all others wanted to be like during the fourth, fifth, and sixth grades. At school I was somebody, not alone, worthy of love. *I love you. Do you love me?* We always checked the yes box.

The "blue house", our single-level ranch home, stood sentry, the last house on the street which ended at the edge of a field. The neighbors all knew each other and, except for the man across the street who hated everyone's dogs, everyone got along well. So, when a prowler began causing difficulties in the neighborhood, everyone banded together to solve the problem. Kind of an early version of today's Neighborhood Watch.

The daring prowler stole meat from garage freezers. He jimmied doors and windows open, showing no regard for hiding his blatant break-ins. When my parents left for an evening out, a crash in the garage interrupted the TV show they left us watching in lieu of a babysitter. My little brother, sisters, and I rushed to the kitchen. We watched, paralyzed, as chips of wood, chiseled from the garage side of the kitchen door, fell to the floor, the resulting hole reaching closer and closer to the doorknob. Reality finally punched through our dazed fear and we fled out the sliding glass door to the next-door neighbor's house.

Another night, when two neighborhood girls slept outside, they claimed to have seen the prowler leaving our garage. They also claimed to have seen my stepfather come out after him. When questioned about whether the first man they saw might not also have been Gene, they giggled and were quite certain.

"Oh, no! Gene was naked!"

After the sighting, the men of the neighborhood intensified their efforts to catch the guy. Since our house was the most frequent target, my stepfather installed a ship's horn on the roof, with a switch by his bed, a burglar alarm. A blaring, loud, discordant blast that, contrary to intent, was only heard in laughing demonstrations. (When it was actually needed, he never flipped the switch.) The men took turns in two's or three's, lying in wait on dark, sloped roofs in the black of night. But all their vigils ever yielded was a large German Shepherd slinking in the shadows. When Gene shot the dog with a blow-dart gun, the dog didn't even yelp. He slipped deeper into the darkness.

The most terrifying event happened in my own bedroom. Lying awake in the middle of the night I stared into the darkness broken only by scattered intrusions from a nearby streetlamp. My bedroom suddenly filled with swarms of flying bugs. I knew they couldn't be real. Fear tugged at my imagination; my skin crawled. Then, through the open door, a dog loomed large. He stood erect on his hind legs, his nose lifted high sniffing the darkened room. Danger glinted off his luminescent teeth. His fur shimmered as the streetlight sent narrow shafts of illumination into the darkness. I couldn't breathe.

He can't be real! He can't be real!

I pulled the blankets over my head. Heat emanated from Rhonda sleeping next to me in the double bed. I pulled the blankets tighter.

In the next instant, Rhonda erupted. Screaming. Kicking. Fear swallowed me in a single gulp. I screamed and kicked too, battering the blankets against the threat of the dog's jagged teeth.

Mom and Gene finally stumbled into our bedroom. Mom's toe had caught in the bedspread, tripping her as she jumped from her sleep to investigate the ruckus. When I heard their voices, I sat upright, untangled myself from the blankets and stared at the open doorway. Rhonda still thrashed and sobbed. Hysteria wrapped her in a straitjacket of fright. The dog was gone. The bugs were gone. There had been no discordant blast from the foghorn.

Rhonda choked broken sobs. "He … he covered my face. He … grabbed … picking me up! I thought he was going to kill me!"

The front door had been left wide open in the attacker's escape.

The mystery of the dog niggled our imaginations. Like the morbid desire of passing motorists to view the gory details of an accident, our nighttime intruder did not arouse fear, but rather an insidious curiosity. We wanted to see him, touch him, dissect him like a bug. We all debated his genus, his habits, his potential identity. The favorite theory was the one the neighborhood kids concocted: "Maybe it's a man dressed up in a dog suit!" After the apparent attempted kidnapping of my sister, it was time for deeper scrutiny. My parents called the police.

I still remember the names of the two detectives: Sergeant Drennan and Detective Stahn. They sat in our living room wearing dark suits and solemn faces, straight out of the television series "Dragnet." The thrill of answering their questions mirrored the drama of the crime series episodes. The police searched the nearby fields. In their pervading presence, we grew confident the danger would no longer taunt our neighborhood.

At last, the prowler was apprehended. He lived just one street over from us. As it turned out, he was a convicted kidnapper. They found a dog suit in his garage.

Genus and species identified, the dried-up carcass of the mystery was brushed aside. Without the distraction, I faced the same empty balloon as before, though by now, its pliable form lay dry, cracked, and shredded at my feet. In its place, my stepfather loomed, like another threatening dog with luminescent teeth. I flinched at his proximity, not knowing whether he would nuzzle … or bite.

That fear and confusion grew as I grew. My body had tasted the early morsels of menses, not to mention other symptoms of blossoming womanhood. That flower was blooming, and I hadn't quite turned ten. My stepfather constantly stepped up to the plate at the slightest indication of my discomfort or injury. When he touched me, "evaluating injuries", my body shook with uncontrollable responses. I hated it because I hated him. And yet, I sought out other ways to feel those sensations. I hid in my dark secrets, fearing naked ugliness in their exposure. With the distance and lack of communication from Mom, I blindly grew up creating my own definitions for all that was going on.

When I was still just ten years old, we traveled for an overnight visit to my aunt and uncle's house in Gridley. While the parents slept behind closed doors, all of us kids sprawled in sleeping bags across the living room floor. In the middle of the night, my cousin Buddy, now a full-grown teenager, gently awakened me.

"Do you know about the birds and the bees?" he asked.

In my naiveté and not realizing he might be talking about anything other than real birds and real bees, I whispered back, "Yes."

"Do you want to do it?"

"Okay," I whispered again, not knowing what I was agreeing to.

Buddy slithered into my sleeping bag, grabbed the top of my underpants and yanked them completely off. Shocked, I lay still, frozen with confusion yet not wanting to appear ignorant. He quickly disposed of his own tidy-whities and plopped face down on top me. He forced his knees between mine and ripped away any remaining shred of my virtue not broken in our first encounter. My silent scream caught in my throat. I was too stunned to move or even think. Buddy disappeared before my choked protests even thought of escaping.

I stared into the silent darkness, my thoughts jumbled. I knew just enough to be afraid I might be pregnant; though I wasn't quite sure I understood the connection. In fact, I spent the next month living in fear, worrying how in the world I would tell my mother.

"Mom, there's a baby in my tummy." I pictured myself, only ten years old, a swollen belly, revealing my plight. I couldn't possibly imagine what would happen next. I wasn't angry with Buddy, nor did I feel any remorse. Basically, I really didn't know any better and, after a few weeks, the thoughts and feelings passed; my tummy remained flat.

ଔ   ଔ   ଔ   ଔ   ଔ

After three years, our blue-house neighborhood grew tedious for Gene. Like a movie watched over and over again, he tired of the plot. The same people. The same action. The repeating script no longer held him. He moved our family to the foothills of the Sierra Nevadas, to China Hill Road outside of El Dorado, near where he had spent his younger days.

He and my mom purchased a two-acre piece of property on a gentle hillside scattered with scrub oaks. Plans for our new home unfolded in our fantasies, materialized in drawings and floor plans. Like waiting for a flower to bloom, we were giddy with anticipation. In the meantime, we rented a very small but temporary house just half a mile from our dreams.

By now there were six children, five girls and one boy. All of us shared a single large bedroom in the one-and-a-half-bedroom country house. Because we knew it was only for a short time, we happily claimed privacy by calling out, "Don't look!" All parties respectfully complied.

My brother, sisters, and I rode horses in exchange for work across the dirt road at the rustic riding stables there, backed by a small lake. The stable owners also allowed us to take a rowboat out on the lake. I loved the lake at night under a canopy of stars, an escape into a world of my own imaginations. The dark, still water whispered to me when it nipped at the oars and lapped at the sides of the old wooden boat. Frogs croaked a moonlight symphony—unfortunately to their own peril—Gene taught us how to gig frogs. Yes. Frog legs do dance in the frying pan and taste just like chicken.

We all worked at clearing brush from the proposed home site. When we burned the brush, poison oak struck back with a painful vengeance. We'd never confronted this demon before. Mom's face swelled so badly, her eyes were mere slits. Solid welts tormented me from head to foot. I sometimes took a hairbrush to my arms in a desperate attempt to appease the god of itching. The doctor recommended baths in colloidal oatmeal, the best treatment available at the time.

Gene taught me some things about drafting and, at nearly twelve years old, I proudly drew the basic plans for the entire second story of our new home. Even a nearby brush fire did little to dampen the family's enthusiasm. But what the fire could not do, the bank did. Two and a half miles of dirt road was the bank's excuse for denying the financing of the family's dreams.

Just a few weeks later, Gene's long-standing job in the aerospace industry fell victim to cutbacks in government spending and the resulting mass layoffs. Everything came crashing down around us.

ೞ   ೞ   ೞ   ೞ   ೞ

6 – The Crush of Darkness

"The shared secret and the shared denial are the most
horrible aspects of incest."
John Bradshaw

I liked our family car, the Corvair. Was it a bit small for
a family with six kids? You bet! But there were always fights over
which two or three of us would squeeze into the small space
behind the back seat. I learned to drive in that Corvair even
though I was only twelve years old. Mom and Dad often had me
drive my brother and sisters the two miles of dirt road to the
school bus stop. I first listened to the Beatles on the car radio in
that Corvair. *"She loves you, yeah, yeah, yeah ...,"* *"I want to hold
your ha-a-a-and ..."* But the Corvair didn't take kindly to the
even-longer dirt road, Sand Ridge Road, even further south off
Highway 49, further away from the town of El Dorado, further
away from civilization. Why the even smaller Renault Dauphin
was a better choice, I never understood. But it became our "other
car," as opposed to the more-frequently-used pickup with a
camper shell. In the pickup, all of us kids piled in the back and
braced ourselves around the turns. My first case of carsickness
struck while riding in that camper shell. I also first saw our new

house while riding in the cab of that pickup, while Mom drove the smaller car with the younger kids.

We crossed a bridge over a river you could wade across in the summer. That was the one good thing about Sand Ridge Road. We spent many sweltering days cooling off, and diving into one of the deeper pools off one of the bigger rocks. California summers demanded such escapes when the house, if you can call it a house, didn't have electricity.

It wasn't a house. Not a real house by my standards. The gray cement block walls looked like a prison. The sound of the broom sweeping the bare plywood floors made my teeth hurt and gave me chills, like that screeching-fingernails-over-a-chalkboard chills. The six of us kids still shared two sets of bunk-beds, but at least they were divided over two bedrooms, privacy callouts still required. A couple of kerosene lamps sat atop Mom's piano. It was on that very piano bench and by the dim light of those lamps that I finally had a conversation with my Mom about obtaining my first bra, long overdue, in addition to my first store-bought dress for a school dance. The junior high school was hiring a live band for the first time and the principal sent a letter home to all the parents requesting the students dress a little nicer than usual for this auspicious occasion.

I'm not sure where the money came from. Most of our clothes had always come from hand-me-downs and, ever since Gene lost his job, we only shopped at thrift stores. This time though, Mom bought me the most adorable sailor dress, navy blue with big white collar and navy trim and a sharp little red tie at the neck, along with nylon stockings, a garter belt, and a size 34B bra.

Not everything at night happened in the light of the kerosene lamps. At least half the time, we ran a generator to power our lights. Once, somebody poured sugar in the gas tank and we had to use those lamps several nights in a row. But for the most part, the family, and sometimes the neighbors, gathered around our well-lit dining table in the evenings playing card games, like Pinochle or Canasta, late into the nights.

Just outside our back door stood a very small water tower, a galvanized tank on a platform of poles, supported at a height just above the roof. Water filled it, pumped from a well at the bottom of the hill. The well water was high in iron, so everyone's teeth turned orange. Not only that, but to get the orange well water up into the "tower" and available to the house, we had to hike down the hill and start the water pump with a pull-chord, like a lawnmower. Gene usually made two of us kids go together to do it, often after dark. Terrified of attacks by bears that frequented a nearby dump, we held our breaths all the way down the hill. Our flashlight beam bounced off every rock and tree and pierced each shadow. We looked frontwards and backwards and jumped at every crack of a twig, hoot of an owl, or pair of red eyes glaring from a bush. We fired up the pump, then ran as fast as we could up the hill until we fell through our front door and slammed it shut behind us … repeating the scenario to turn off the pump at bedtime.

Being now in the tumultuous time of junior high, life on Sand Ridge Road wreaked havoc for me. Kids at school teased me about my orange teeth and unshaved legs. Mom, with smooth skin and light hair didn't need to shave her own legs. To my unfortunate and intense dismay, she forbade me, her only dark-haired daughter, to shave mine. Once I tried to sneak my stepfather's razor and shave my legs in the bathtub. But the generator, keeping our lights on that night, suddenly shut off and I lost a three-inch strip of skin off the front of my shin.

There were only four other families that lived up Sand Ridge Road. We couldn't see any of their houses from our hilltop due to the many oak trees and overgrowth of the general brush that covered those Sierra foothills. Telephone service had not migrated out that far, so socializing with the neighbors had to be very intentional. Fortunately, they all intended it a lot, and I even earned quite a few babysitting jobs in the process.

Our lives grew dismal, both for our family and for the country at large. I remember the day in November, just before Thanksgiving, walking in the outdoor corridors of my school. Everyone else sat in classrooms behind closed doors. It was quiet. I breathed in the fresh air while I avoided rushing back to class after dropping paperwork off at the office. The principal's voice crackled over the speakers. He did not usually broadcast to everyone like that, so I froze in my tracks and tipped my head up to listen. President John F. Kennedy had been assassinated. His voice broke as he relayed the news to us all. A weight in my chest plummeted to my leaden feet, which could not move. After a moment, a door opened nearby. Cries echoed before the door slammed and one of the teachers ran to the office. No more lessons were taught that day. We mostly cried and waited for the school busses to take us home through a world that was no longer safe. And yet, our lives continued on.

Gene cut firewood for a living and he dragged me along to help split the logs with a maul and wedge. He also taught me to drive the gnarly, old tractor. Our family's survival depended on my constant hard work with him. Just before an eighth-grade field trip to the Capitol, I sprained my ankle while traipsing down a hillside behind him, and then had to traverse the class journey on crutches.

In the winter of '64, constant heavy rains flooding the west made the three-and-a-half miles of our dirt road nearly impassable. The bridge connecting Sand Ridge Road to the highway grew increasingly precarious. When the approach to the bridge finally crashed into the raging waters, each of the five families living on our hill was caught with a vehicle on either side of the bridge … except us. Both our Chevy pickup and the Renault Dauphin were parked in the mucky surroundings of the unfinished cement-block house.

Gene, along with the other men, hauled a couple of large planks down to the bridge. He dared to drive the truck across the narrow planks, while everyone held their breath, so that we, too, had a vehicle on either side. The men then moved the planks together. When we had to drive into town, we drove the Renault down to the river, parking it a safe distance from the disintegrating riverbanks. One by one, we walked across the planks, like a tightrope to the bridge, terrified at the angry turbid waters convulsing below. Only one person at a time was allowed to walk across the bridge. That way, if the entire bridge finally gave way, only one person would be lost. We each breathed a great sigh of relief upon reaching the safety of the other side. Then we all piled into the pickup, protected by the camper shell, and drove the winding long drive into town.

As muddy hillsides gave way to spring, Grandma Westin, my mother's mother, arrived for a visit. It had been obvious from the beginning of Mom's second marriage that Grandma Westin did not like our new stepfather. In the middle of her visit, which was supposed to last several days, I woke up during the night to the sound of angry voices. I listened without paying much attention until I heard my stepfather mention my name.

Grandma Westin snapped in response, "Yeah, feel her up … she's got two good points!"

Silence crashed. I lay there horrified at the words just spoken about me. Grandma was gone the next morning. A semblance of peace settled on the household, but my world had been shaken by the exchange.

A few nights later, asleep on my upper bunk, I awoke to Gene standing next to my bed, his face just inches from mine. Sheer terror pinned me to the bed in silence as he removed the blankets and pushed me into a nightmare beyond my darkest imaginations. He touched. He tasted. He plundered. Exposed and defiled, I pretended to still sleep, begged the darkness to swallow me. But my body betrayed me. The nightmare stretched on … until he left … slipped quietly from my bedroom.

Alone on my upper bunk, confusion crept in. Pieces of comprehension punched into my mind, like an embroidery needle piercing through fabric, stitch by stitch, until an ugly pattern emerges. A mistake. The wrong colors. This isn't what it's supposed to look like. Anger smoldered, then fear, then shame … shame in the conflicting emotions of demons awakened who should have slept years longer.

The next morning, I stumbled to the breakfast table. He sat at the end of the table, in his usual spot, and sipped his steaming coffee. The memory of the nightmare swamped me. Voices around the table blurred in my head. Vomit stuck in my throat. He offered me pancakes.

And so, the ruse began. I struggled in the grip of immobilizing terror, my face a facade as though nothing had happened. He, too, carried on as though everything was normal. That was the beginning of my utter hatred of him.

The door had been opened. His nighttime visits became a regular occurrence. As with the first time, the experience was incomprehensible to my young mind. I knew what was happening was wrong. Self-condemnation permeated every fiber of my being, but I was powerless in its grip.

I could not go to my mother. In the first place, what would Mom do? Nothing! She had always done nothing when the children suffered at his hands in the past. In the second place, there was no mother-daughter relationship to form the basis for a conversation. I was caught in a world over which I had no control.

At school, I stuffed it. I buried it all, hid it deep in the recesses of my mind where it couldn't reach out and rip at my now fragile identity. Struggling for self-value, it was more important than ever that I get A's in every class. I needed my teachers to recognize goodness in me.

Please, my heart begged, *tell me I'm good.*

First in line, best in class, even asking my teachers for verbal commendations.

"You don't have to come up to me for comments on your work every day," Mrs. Rickner stated in front of my eighth-grade social studies classroom. "You'll get your grades and my comments on your paper when you're finished. You're all doing wonderful work and we'll discuss it together." Her smile shone equally for each student.

My face burned, and bile stuck in my throat. *She's talking to me. I know she's talking to me. I'm not good. I'm a bother.*

Please, my heart begged, *somebody tell me I'm good.*

I sat at the lunch table with the popular girls. I laughed at their jokes. But then Carol—Carol with the long dark hair and angelic voice—turned to me, her eyes squinting. "Why do you always go 'ha, ha, ha, ha, ha' at everything we say?"

The air pounded around me, smothered me until the voices were jumbled echoes bouncing off cavernous prison walls. Laughing giant faces and sneering lips flared in my hot eyes. My sandwich frothed in my throat, fighting for release.

I can't let them see me cry.

Each day I sat quiet and alone in the school bus for the hour-long ride to the bridge at Sand Ridge Road. The bus driver, a loud and boisterous man when other kids were on the bus, became lecherously quiet when they were all dropped at their stops. Then he watched me with piercing eyes in the mirror. His tongue wet his lips. I knew what men did with those lips. I squeezed my books to my chest and slouched down in the seat. I hid my body from him. If I didn't look at him then his eyes couldn't touch me. I looked down at the floor as I slipped past him … as I escaped the bus.

I stood alone on the empty bridge. Behind me, the old yellow bus headed back up Highway 49. Ahead of me, the dusty road climbed to the cement block house and my lonely, recurring nightmare.

ೞ ೞ ೞ ೞ ೞ

7 – The Hauser Curse

"To those who abuse: the sin is yours, the crime is yours,
and the shame is yours."
Flora Jessop

I hope Mrs. Rickner, my eighth-grade Social Studies, English, and Drama teacher, knew what a powerful influence she had on my life. I hope more middle school teachers recognize the opportunities they have to touch young lives … to have an impact on future adults. She was barely an adult herself. She and her husband had worked their way through college by working at Disneyland. This Disneyland alumni brought magic with her. For our eighth-grade Christmas play, she gave us no script, merely an outline, and we learned improvisation. In my lead role as an elf, I thrived. I became more than myself. I could flourish and be somebody at school, even if I couldn't at home.

To an insecure eighth grader, she saw me as I could be … at least at school. She challenged me to be the best that I could be. She gave me a B on one of my papers, when I knew, and everyone else knew, that my report was the best in the classroom. Others got A's. Frustrated and dejected, I asked her about it.

"Yes," she replied. "Yours is the best in the class. But it's not the best that you can do."

She made a difference. That singular action changed the entire rest of my school life, and even work projects thereafter. I no longer did just enough to be better than everyone else in my class, but I genuinely strove to be the best that I could be.

It's truly a shame I could not apply that attitude to my own evaluations of myself as a person. I set expectations so high that I always fell short. I had the expectation that I could be perfect in all things, but I could not be perfect in my response to my stepfather ... and to what little remnant of understanding I had about God. I was a sinner!

My good grades and work performance were a sham, a façade. I had to be the best, so I could hide the ugliness inside. I continued to push the ugliness deep, to hide my sin.

Mrs. Rickner saw good in me, even if I could no longer find it. When our family moved into Placerville, out of our school district and before year's end, Mrs. Rickner volunteered to drive me to school each day. She lived not too far from us. As a result, I graduated junior high with my class, and with the Salutatorian status I had earned by my good grades.

But eighth grade ended. My relationship with Mrs. Rickner ended. I was left to fend for myself and there was no one to teach me how to navigate the waters. I flailed on my own.

About this time, Gene began talking about the "Hauser Curse." His family, Hauser, now my last name too, had feuded with another clan back in his grandfather's day in the state of Kansas. The old woman and matriarch of the other clan had uttered a curse on the Hauser family. Bad luck would follow them wherever they went. The events and downfalls in our lives were evidence to that fact, starting with the death of his first wife during childbirth.

The prowler in Orangevale, the loss of his job and dreams, the floods on Sand Ridge Road ... all pointed to the curse. And it was not over. That very summer, while trying to light a barbecue with gasoline, it blew up on Gene and burned his arm badly. Mom rushed him to the hospital. He came home with blisters the size of golf balls all over his right arm. Then one day while I was washing dishes, I picked up a heavy aluminum pot off the electric stove, with wet hands. The electrocution tossed me clear across the room, bashed me up against the counter and down onto the floor. I sat stunned, wondering what in the world had happened.

Yes, the Hauser curse was alive and well in our new house in Placerville, California.

Well, it wasn't exactly a new house. It was an old Victorian, built in 1892, the same year my Grandma Westin was born. With a big stone wall and a hillside separating the house from Highway 50 below, the peeling white paint and stone walkways heralded its days past. French doors and worn hardwood floors lent the home warmth and character. And, of course, there were the secret hide-a-ways and passages in addition to a dirt cellar right through a door in the kitchen. The wooden stairway to the second floor, where only girls slept now, was narrow with a landing half-way up where the stairs made a complete 180-degree turn. My brother slept in the leg of the L-shaped living room, which had been barricaded for him for privacy. That's why his sudden appearance at my bedside in the middle of the night one night was such a shock and another casualty of the Hauser curse. My parents had abandoned us for an overnight tryst at the casinos in South Lake Tahoe. We were left to fend for ourselves.

"Deb, wake up," he whispered while urgently shaking my shoulder. "Somebody is downstairs."

I bolted upright and heard the muffled banging and clanking as someone dug around in the cupboards and drawers downstairs. I sucked in a big gulp of fear while Richie also shook Rhonda awake on the bottom bunk. Both climbed into the top bunk with me. We pulled the covers tight around our necks and strained to hear what was going on. The bedframe nearly rattled from our own frightful shaking.

Then we heard his footsteps on the stairs. Step. Step. Step. He paused at the landing. We held our breaths and I thought I might throw up. Then, another step up. Step. Step. Step. Halfway up the second set of steps, he stopped. The darkness crushed us and by now the bed was soaking wet from what I hoped was just sweat. Fear hung in the air, and we pressed tighter together. Then his footsteps descended, down, until the sounds disappeared completely.

For a seeming eternity of minutes, we dared not move and barely breathed. Finally convinced he left the house, we spilled out of the bed, and all three of us clambered into the bathroom together, forgetting any thoughts about privacy. Richie could not bring himself to go back downstairs, so we all crowded back into my upper bunk. We awoke early next morning when Gene hollered at us from downstairs about leaving the kitchen door open to the outside.

Not long after the break-in, I started high school at the old El Dorado High School sprawled atop the Canal Street hill in Placerville, the very same high school my stepfather attended in his early days. It was a grand school of old brick buildings, steeped in traditions, and a great cafeteria such as I hadn't experienced before. I couldn't understand why I had to take algebra, but I did like our Christmas art class project: painting windows throughout the old downtown businesses. I never sat through a Cougar's football game, but I did enjoy the pre-game spirit bonfires. I had a crush on Mark Elliott who lived in the big red Victorian just down the street from our house, but it was his friend I first kissed at a bonfire.

Part way through the school year, I "fell in love" with Dennis. (Well, "in love" as much as a fourteen-year-old can presume.) Quiet and brooding, and often sharing his thoughts about suicide, he told me he loved me. No one except Grandpa Max had ever told me that before. The smell of his black leather jacket enveloped me when he held me close. He said I was the only one he could really talk to. So, when my parents announced we were planning another move, this time to San Jose, I grew very concerned when Dennis, overwhelmed with sadness at my pending departure, suddenly disappeared from my life. Just before I left though, I caught a glimpse of him on the other side of the cafeteria with another girl enveloped in his black leather jacket. Hmph! So much for true love. I was ready to leave, guilt free and good riddance!

The San Jose move was happening quickly. A mapmaking company there had hired my stepfather. I was mortified, however, when Gene announced that he, my brother, and I would go down a week ahead of the family to paint the new house and make it ready. Mom would follow later with the younger children. So far, my stepfather's activities had been discreet and without acknowledgment between us. Now I was being thrown into a totally exposed and unprotected situation. My brother would be there, which could possibly prevent any blatant activities. But he was young. Horrifying scenarios assaulted my mind.

The painting began without incident. Once the drop cloths and masking tape were stripped away, I opened my eyes each morning to the soft powder blue of my new bedroom walls. As I stepped from my bed, my toes touched the floor. I no longer slept in a bunk bed. Morning sun poured through my bedroom window. My apprehensions melted in the euphoria of my new surroundings.

But my euphoria was dashed when, at last, towards the end of the week, my stepfather slipped into my room in the middle of the night. I played my usual game of pretending to be asleep, and he pretended to believe that I was. But the stakes were higher now. I was alone, my bed much closer to the floor. I sickened at the realization as his body pressed into mine and the final deed nearly tripped into completion. Shocked into a guilt greater than I could bear, I cried out for my mother. Gene abruptly pulled back. Shaking, I pretended the cry had merely been a disturbance of my sleep. He allowed me this charade and shared in its shrouded secrets.

Oh, but the guilt lingered. It engulfed and entangled me beyond reparation. Is it truly rape when the body responds with craving desire? The questions and the feelings tormented me. Unfulfilled demons of desire tore at my senses of right and wrong. Yet I had to walk through my days in obedience to an elusive morality.

Why did you do this to me?

I needed to be seen as good. I needed to see me as good. Certainly there was a Hauser curse, and now that curse was mine.

Somebody, please tell me I'm good.

Can one be good when filled with hate and torment ... and self-contempt?

CR   CR   CR   CR   CR

8 – The Edge of Dusk

"I pushed God away. I hid him in the recesses of my mind."
D.H. Silva

"There are childhoods that have been so bleak as to seem only tragic." That was written by John Eldredge in his Sacred Romance Workbook and Journal. That is how I look back and view my own childhood: an entire segment of my life stolen from me; a childhood devoid of innocence, delight, and parental love and guidance.

In the emotional abandonment, I felt worthless. With the lack of any adult guidance or communication, I was left to develop my own definitions for things happening in my life and around me. Those misshaped definitions included a sense of right and wrong, a sense of God and judgment, a sense of sin. It was that sense of pervading sin, and darkness, that colored the events of my life yet to follow. A sense of being ugly before God.

I clung to optimism, unwilling to believe my stepfather had impacted my life in ways that threatened even my sanity. I accepted my perceptions, my shattered boundaries, and moral understandings as normal. I didn't know anything different. Perhaps recognition was delayed by the compassion showed me in the aftermath of the experience, when I came down with rheumatic fever at the end of my freshman year. Looking back, I wonder if the rheumatic fever was a psychosomatic illness, a way to hide from the reality of the abuse, my confusing emotions and guilt in the aftermath of the abuse. But the symptoms of the disease were very real.

I sprained my ankle, but I didn't know when or how. It hurt. My parents wrapped it in an elastic bandage but had to add another one further up the leg when pain wracked my knee. The next day, when they had to wrap my other ankle and knee, and energy drained from my body, they took me to a chiropractor. He prescribed massive doses of vitamins. Though I gained some strength from the vitamin regime, the chiropractor admitted my condition was more than he could handle. He referred us to a heart doctor who diagnosed my illness as rheumatic fever.

Unable to attend school, I spent most of my time lying on the couch. Pain and weakness in my joints hobbled my walking. I had no energy and my heart often raced. My stepfather also had rheumatic fever as a teenager, so this became a point of empathy, perhaps even redemption, as he showered me with care and compassion, devoid of sexual overtones.

The neighborhood kids, along with my own brother and sisters, often visited me as I lay helpless on the couch. They brought games to play and books to read. I savored the attention, willing to accept any and all care available to me—like a healing bandage on my broken life.

As dusk fell one evening, the usual group of neighborhood kids brought a book describing supernatural experiences. I read the stories aloud with feigned suspense. The pallid beams from the setting sun faded into darkness until it was no longer light enough to see the pages. The mood evaporated when my brother switched on the lights. The kids ran outside to play in the warm evening, while our parents visited together next door. They left me alone with the carrion of the tales.

Fascination haunted me with the story of the man who spoke to a pencil. He held the pencil lightly, asked a question, and the pencil spelled out the answer. Compelled, I picked up a pencil and notepad from the coffee table and sat upright. Pencil poised, a frayed corner of the cream-colored living-room drapes drew my focus. I stared. The crisscross weave magnified into roads of threads dividing deep canyons. My mind searched for a question. A picture of George emerged in my consciousness. George, the beautiful boy just one street away, a David McCallum look-alike, secret agent Illya Kuryakin in the television series "The Man from U.N.C.L.E." A warm blush washed over my face.

"Does George love me?"

Deafening silence filled the room. My illness-weakened heart pounded hard against my chest. The pencil moved in my hand. My blood burned hot and the room started spinning. I trembled as it continued its self-directed motion. Then it stopped. My heart stood still. My breath caught in my throat.

"Yes." The pencil spelled, "Yes."

I gasped. It wasn't for the answer itself but rather for the fact that there was an answer. Nearly hyperventilating, I stumbled and crawled to the front door. I screamed at the kids playing on the front lawn. Frightened by my hysteria, they ran to fetch my parents.

Gene snatched me up and settled me back on the couch. Mom, red-faced and mouth set, grabbed and thrust the book into its owner's hands.

"Get that out of here!" She growled. He ran. "And you," she glared at me. "You stop this nonsense."

I tried to explain but she refused to hear it. She didn't believe me. Just like she didn't believe me those many years ago when the cats invaded my bedroom, when Rhonda was still a baby. I lay awake in the middle of the night and our neighbor's fluffy, gray tabby jumped through the window by my bed. A second cat followed, but I didn't recognize him. Both cats bounded across the foot of my bed and jumped into Rhonda's crib. Rhonda erupted in screaming wails. The cats scampered out of her crib, scurried across my bed, and jumped back out the window. Grandma Westin was visiting at the time, and she and mom burst through the bedroom door.

"What happened?" Mom demanded as she flipped on the light switch.

I covered my eyes with my arm. I gulped in air as I choked out in crying sobs, "The cats. They jumped in the window, then jumped on Rhonda."

"There are no cats. What did you do?" Mom's glaring eyes loomed over me while Grandma stood by the door, arms crossed.

"I didn't do anything," I pleaded.

Mom banged her fist on the wall by the window. "The window is closed!"

Grandma shook her head and stomped out of the room.

"But I saw …"

Mom picked up the still-crying Rhonda, wrapped in her blanket, and walked away. "That's enough from you, Deborah Joan," she snarled.

The walls shook when she slammed the door.

Now, once again, she didn't believe me. Like with the cats, she dismissed me.

The next day, burning curiosity begged me to pick up that pencil again. Simple questions. Simple answers. Then, it interrupted me, drew a row of adjoined humps, changed direction and traced a second row of humps above the first, finished with three humps, almost a tail, above the second row. It interrupted me several times with the same drawing. Each time it outlined the exact same number of humps each direction.

"What is this drawing?" Reason eluded me. Nothing else existed behind the closed doors of my blue bedroom.

"It is me," the pencil spelled.

For the next two days, I conversed with the pencil. Sometimes it interrupted with, "I have to go now." And for a time, it stood motionless between my thumb and fingers. Then it returned, dancing on nerve impulses.

It told me of a power greater than itself, a power it was subject to. It told me that just like each person has a guardian angel, they also have a "guardian devil." The conversation grew too intense to keep to myself.

I had to tell my mom. Even if she didn't believe me at first. I had to make her listen.

I finally told her. Whether she believed me or not, I'm not sure, but both my parents worried about the toll it might be taking on my illness. They spoke to my heart doctor in an effort to require me to stop the "ridiculous pencil conversations." The doctor, however, referred us to Stanford University where they were researching psychic and telekinetic powers.

At Stanford, I sat alone in a small white room. Everything around me gleamed white. Even the air oozed white coldness. I watched my reflection in the large window that filled one of the walls. I couldn't see through it, but I knew they were watching me. My stomach was in my throat, my breaths shallow. Maybe I just imagined the pencil. Maybe it moved because I wanted it to and subconsciously moved it myself.

A single doctor entered the room, a faceless man in a long white coat. He sat down across from me. "So, tell me about the pencil."

I told my story matter-of-factly, careful to not sensationalize anything, convinced he would chastise me, admonish me to stop trying to gain attention with such foolishness. But, to my surprise, after affirming events like these were often associated with major illnesses, the interviewer encouraged me to continue. They wanted to observe and study me.

Back at home and feeling important, emboldened to step out further with my supernatural confidante, I probed deeper. I asked if I could have visual contact.

"Yes." But there were very specific instructions. Exactly at midnight, it told me to say "Debbie, come now." But, I could not tell anybody about it afterwards or, the pencil warned, "You will die."

Hesitant, and frightened, I asked, "Is there any way to break the spell?"

"Yes", it responded. "Pray to God."

I hurled the pencil across the room, ripped the pages into shreds, stuffed them into the trash can like smoldering embers too hot to handle. I backed myself up to the wall, my knees up to my chest, and sat in stunned silence, emotions drained, and waited for fear to take flight.

There was God again. Was He taunting me? Had I tread too far onto evil ground? The pictures of Jesus that I loved when I was six years old, smiling at the children, were too far away from the realities of my existence. This God was a judging God and I was sure my sin was great. I could not stand in His light. I thought of the burning bush in the story of Moses and feared I was too close to the flames. Maybe that's why I was sick in the first place. He was punishing me.

My rheumatic fever turned out to be a light case. I only remained in bed for about a month. By the fourth quarter of my freshman year, I was fully recovered, able to attend school and even able to participate in P.E. I would have to take penicillin for a few years to prevent recurrences resulting from strep infections. It also left me with a minor heart murmur. Other than reduced stamina, and having to wear clunky orthopedic shoes, my life continued as any other normal teenager. Fortunately for my social standings, nobody enforced the wearing of the orthopedic shoes beyond the end of my freshman year.

I pushed God away, hid Him in the dark recesses of my mind, and determined to live my life worthy of the recognition of others … needing the recognition of others. God was not my problem. It was people I needed to impress.

CR   CR   CR   CR   CR

9 – The Search for Significance

*"What you think about yourself matters more than
what others think about you."*
Sandeep Maheshwari

"I thought he was going to kill me," my little sister
Rhonda confided to me years later. "I was only five years old
when he made me go into the bathroom with him. Mom wasn't
home. But when we lived on Sand Ridge Road …" Her voice
broke. "I thought he was going to kill me. He made me get in the
truck with him. I didn't want to go. But he made me."

Rhonda bit back her tears. Determination grabbed hold
and she sat up straighter, stiffened her shoulders. "When we
turned up the dirt road, he made me take off my pants. He made
me lay across his lap while he was driving … and he … I didn't
know what to do … all the way home … I thought he was going
to kill me and leave my body in the woods. So, I did what he
said."

Rhonda was only ten years old when we lived on Sand
Ridge Road. We each had our own secrets too terrible to share,
too ashamed to share. We both thought we were alone. For
Rhonda, it was the fear of reprisal; for me, the straitjacket of
shame. Both muzzles hid the truth.

So many times, we think we are the only ones experiencing emotionally destructive pain. Nobody can understand what we are going through. But that is a lie. As long as evil hides in the darkness, it thrives. Like mold and bacteria in a dark warm place, it spreads and it destroys. We didn't know how to bring it to the light. We suffered under the weight of our own inadequacies.

When we moved to San Jose, the change of location, the allure of a new home and a new life inspired both of us. Ready to shuck our shared distaste for feeling worthless, unpopular, and residing on the bottom rung of the social ladder, Rhonda and I made a pact: we were going to be somebody! We needed to prove, if only to ourselves, we were people of value. The beginning of that road for me, unfortunately, was a precipitous detour.

"Are you afraid?" my new friend Gloria taunted. She flung her long, black, kinky hair back over her bare olive shoulders. "How do you think I got this sexy red tube top and matching lipstick? My momma don't give me that much allowance." She pursed her lips like she was kissing the air. "Come on." She grabbed my arm and we strode laughing into the drugstore.

Gloria smiled and fluttered her eyelashes at the middle-aged man behind the cash register. His eyes widened from behind his thick eyeglasses. Beads of sweat glistened on his bald head.

"I need to buy flashlight batteries for my brother," she nearly whimpered to the befuddled man. "I don't know anything about batteries. Can you help me?"

As he led her down a side aisle, she glanced back at me, smiled and nodded her head towards the selection of top 45 records arranged like files in the box at the other end of the front counter. My stomach knotted up, but I had my marching instructions. I didn't want Gloria to think I was a scaredy-cat. She did get on my nerves at times, but she was popular in the neighborhood and I wanted her to like me.

My face burned as I flipped through the black vinyl discs in paper cases. When I saw a Beach Boys title I liked, I pulled the record from the box and quickly slipped it into my large blue purse. Gloria liked Martha and the Vandellas and Marvin Gaye, so I grabbed a couple of those. Then I saw The Beatles. I loved the Beatles! And there was Dead Man's Curve by Jan & Dean. More than half a dozen records were buried deep in my bag before Gloria returned with the clerk and a single battery.

"Oh my gosh," she said laughing as we rounded the corner outside the store. "I was so afraid he was going to turn around and see you. I kept bumping up against his arm to keep his attention. Let me see what you got." Under the shade of a tree, we giggled over our collection.

"We have to come back tomorrow," she cooed, "and I'll bring back this battery and tell him it was the wrong one. I want that new record by Percy Sledge, 'When a Man Loves a Woman.' It is soooo sexy. Did you see it there?"

It had been so easy. Eager to return the next day and increase my own selection of 45's, I happily concurred. My mom didn't give me much of an allowance either. In fact, she didn't give me any allowance. We returned the next day, and the day after that.

The first day I walked to the grocery store without Gloria, I wore a bright-colored shirt with very large pockets. Just after I slipped a small bottle of shampoo into my pocket, I felt the presence of someone behind me. I froze in my tracks and my face burned hot.

"I hope you're planning on paying for that," a deep male voice spoke over my shoulder.

I turned. My face didn't even come up to the man's shoulder. The embroidered name on his green vest, right at my eye level, read "Manager."

"I, uh, forgot to grab a shopping cart." I stumbled through the words as I held up the shampoo bottle for him to see. "I'll go get one." I put the shampoo back on the shelf, slipped past him, and hurried out of the store.

My future self thanked him for catching me … for ending my life of crime right then and there. I avoided Gloria after that, not caring how pretty or popular she was.

I wasn't so bad looking myself. Nearly fifteen years old, I had already achieved my full height, pushing five feet, seven inches. Long, dark brown hair tumbled past my shoulders. I looked like I had stepped off the pages of a teen fashion magazine. In fact, when I cut a picture out of a magazine of a model who resembled me, my mom responded with, "When did you do that?" However, I still struggled to overcome my shyness and insecurities, which is why I had latched onto the gregarious Gloria in the first place.

The heat of August bore down on our neighborhood as the last weeks of summer were wrapping up. My sophomore year of high school at Andrew Hill High would be starting soon and I was eager to begin. I liked school. I liked learning history, and English, and art. I escaped to busy halls of education, to the stimulation of so much happening around me. It was during those last few weeks before school when I fell in love with Ted.

He stood in his open garage as I walked to the grocery store one day. My knees nearly buckled, and butterflies fluttered in my stomach. Straight, sun-bleached hair fell over his face. He turned his head towards me, but his eyes did not meet mine. His skin glistened bronze, like the surfers from Santa Cruz, painted by the California sun. From that first moment, my sole purpose in life became meeting him.

Just a few days later he was playing baseball with his equally attractive, but younger, brother in the schoolyard just over our back fence. Herds of wild horses could not keep me from just happening to wander over there.

Ted and I became an item. Although we attended different high schools, neither of us dated anyone else. We spent much of our non-school time either on the phone or together. Fortunately, both families approved of the relationship. Gene always embarrassed me when Ted called, and he answered the phone, "Kelly's Pool Hall." And, of course, my stepfather had to "test" him with a vice-gripping handshake. Ted managed to hold his own in the "contest" so Gene approved of him as my boyfriend.

Our first date, the high school football game, the moment Ted grasped my hand to cross the street, my heart jumped. For two years, we shared every weekend, and every summer day: football games, dances, junior prom, Santa Cruz beaches, and making out in the back seat at drive-in movies. I daydreamed about weddings and babies and practiced signing my name: "Mrs. Debbie Larson." Ted was my forever love, the Turtles song, "Happy Together," "our song." Nothing in my past could drag me down.

For my junior year, along with half the population of Andrew Hill High School, the district reassigned me to the brand-new Oak Grove High School. I tried out for that very first Song Girl team, AKA Pom-Pom Girls, for the new Eagles sports teams. I endured the grueling practices every day after school, bouncing and dancing, learning the try-out routine, nightly ice packs on my leg muscles, and the promise of cute, short uniforms with the blue and gold pom poms. For tryouts, we strode onto the stage, one at a time. The judging panel consisted of the entire existing football team and the student council. Linda Rich, who had been a pom-pom girl that year, her junior year, was the presumed head song girl for the upcoming year, her senior year. Everyone expected her to win the most points, assuring her of that position.

My turn came up, seventh or eighth in line. I nervously took my position, front knee up, toe pointed, pom poms held at my waist. The music started. I danced. Time for my first kick. Up went my leg, my foot straight above my head. The entire audience gasped, then each hurriedly scribbled on their ballots. I knew I had done well. Unfortunately, perhaps, too well.

The results were announced. I earned more points than Linda Rich. I was the new head song girl. And, of course, that went over like a ton of bricks with those in her circle. A year of conflict followed. She was on the yearbook committee and, for some reason, the yearbook did not list me as "head." She was pictured first. But, somehow, we made it through that year, squad intact.

The Eagles were a lousy football team, but their basketball team was stellar. In the final tournament, it came down to our school and Ted's school. Excitement flared in the final quarter. I danced and yelled my heart out in support of our team. Suddenly, I grew dizzy and nearly fainted. I sat on the lowest bleacher when one of the coaches escorted me down to the end, had me lie down, then hovered over me. The game ended and I had no idea who won. By then, the fire department arrived and a paramedic placed an oxygen mask over my face. The ambulance waited nearby but no one could do anything until my parents arrived. Everything around me blurred and voices echoed as though speaking through water.

My parents finally showed. With their permission, the paramedics lifted me onto the gurney and wheeled me out through the gymnasium doors. Students gathered and chattered, some hands over mouths. The oxygen mask remained with the firemen, and my mom joined me in the back of the ambulance. By the time we rolled through the Emergency Room doors, I was doing fine. Apparently, I had hyper-ventilated. The worst thing they could have done in the situation was give me oxygen!

All in all, my junior year was a good year. Along with another girlfriend, I also interviewed for the school's Teen Fashion Board representative at the Emporium, a large, popular department store. I strode into the interview in a two-piece orange dress suit I sewed myself, topped with a floppy orange hat, my orange fish-net stockings, and my new orange shoes. Orange proved my color of success.

The Teen Fashion Board introduced me to a whole new world. My plans for Stanford University, and a career in commercial design, dissipated in the glamorous appeal of fashion. I enjoyed makeovers, modeling in fashion shows, and participating in other special events for the store. I learned what went on behind the scenes to bring all the latest fashions to the buying public. I discovered opportunities in careers I didn't even know existed. During that year, my career plans in the fashion industry were born.

Revolutionary changes swept our country in those years. The students at the University of Berkeley rioted and burned draft cards in protest of the escalating Viet Nam War. The more violent Black Panthers joined in, wreaking violence wherever they could. The Viet Nam war ripped the fabric of students' expectations everywhere. Right or wrong, there was no good answer. Demonstrations, marches, and riots erupted all over the country.

Across the bay from Berkeley, in San Francisco, the hippies in Haight-Ashbury gathered together proclaiming peace and love, enhancing their experiences with marijuana and LSD. Many of my friends made the weekly weekend sojourns to Haight-Ashbury. It was the cool place to be and be seen.

Terrified of drugs at the time, especially the LSD everyone raved about, I dared not cross that line. I knew if I took their drugs, if LSD touched my tongue, I would plunge into a hallucination, a never-ending nightmare from which there would be no return. I had already proven, during my rheumatic fever, that my mind was too impressionable. It terrified me. I envisioned jumping off a ten-story balcony, as had been reported about a guy high on the drug. My best girlfriend chose drugs and Haight Ashbury; our bonds of friendship shattered.

I bought into the government propaganda, hook, line, and sinker. We had to stop the communists and Viet Nam was where we, the U.S., drew the line and took a stand. They spouted the domino theory: if Viet Nam fell then other countries would fall and communism would be on our doorstep. So, I wasn't protesting anything. There was no need for me to join the throngs in San Francisco or Berkeley.

The summer of 1968, Uncle Sam laid claim to Ted's services. Devastated, I couldn't imagine my life without him. Our final night together, Ted drove me home in his Ford Galaxy. On the way home we stopped, as we usually did, on a deserted street not far from my house. No street lights were installed yet, no structures built, and no one ever bothered us there. I loved Ted with that blinding, consuming love of a sixteen-year-old. It had only been Ted's moral foundation and incredible self-control that had prevented the inevitable from happening— until that night—in the front seat of his Ford Galaxy.

Junior Prom with Ted ... in my homemade red velvet dress.

ભ   ભ   ભ   ભ   ભ

10 – Accidental Prom Queen

"Desire embraced darkness and dressed it in gold."
D.H. Silva

Ted was gone. That same summer, just before my senior year, my parents uprooted us again. Our station wagon headed south. The lush green of the Bay Area faded to the desolation of the Southern California desert. We moved to California City, a public relations land grab promising paradise and prosperity to thousands of buyers who bought thousands of proposed homesites sprawled over desolate hills a twenty-minute drive from the town of Mojave. Fifty years later, it remains thousands of proposed homesites sprawled over desolate hills, the third largest city in the State of California by virtue of its land mass. However, there is now a McDonalds in town.

Emptiness flooded my spirit. On one hand, I experienced relief at leaving Oak Grove High School, a school of snobbish cliques. The thought of continuing leadership of the Song Girl squad mortified me. I still didn't fit in with the kids there. Most of the girls came from fairly well-to-do families. They wore the latest fashions, went on dream vacations, and planned to attend expensive colleges. Song girls and cheerleaders dated football players and basketball stars. I sewed my own clothes, wore hand-me-downs, and shopped at thrift stores. We never went on vacations. I relied on the hope I was smart enough to earn college scholarships. And my boyfriend, Ted, seemed a million miles away now.

I leaned my face against the window glass in the back seat as we drove through the endless farmlands of the San Joaquin Valley. I dug deep for motivation, something to get excited about in the move, but I couldn't grab hold of anything ... except for the tiny morsel of relief at leaving the snobs. The flatlands of the valley ascended the barren mountains of Tehachapi Pass, and I began to desperately miss the color green. Depression downright devoured me when we hit desert sands that didn't even know what green looked like. And California City ... well, not much at all can be said about the vast emptiness, the desert-colored structures placed at regular intervals on the desert-colored sand ... they were called "houses", and one of them was ours. The Rolling Stones' song "Paint It Black" filled my mind and mirrored my emotions.

We lived in poverty in California City, neither parent working. Each week they brought home food boxes from the welfare department filled with enough Spam, instant mashed potatoes, and butter to feed our family of nine. (Another brother had come into the family while we lived in San Jose.) Sandstorms pitted our windshields, lightning bolts stabbed the earth at the drive-in movies, and I wondered over and over again how in the world this move played out the promise of a better family life.

Mojave High School, though boasting terrific school spirit—Go Mustangs!—matriculated only fifty-four students in my senior class. A significant number of those senior girls were already married, and so, too, some juniors. Some even had babies. One girl in my bookkeeping class got married over Thanksgiving vacation and then divorced over Easter vacation.

After-school and weekend activities centered around illegal drag racing on deserted desert roads, hanging out at the recreation center, or, if one was a member of the award-winning Mojave High School marching band, traveling for competitions.

Rhonda became a cheerleader at our new school and dated the most popular boy in her freshman class. I remained aloof, making it clear to everyone I already had a boyfriend, and he was in Viet Nam.

Just before Ted left the U.S. mainland for Viet Nam, he made one visit to our house in California City. I mention it only because it sets the stage for what transpired a few short months later. I was pregnant. Well, convinced I was pregnant, I told my mother that pain punched my abdomen, without mention of my own suspicions. Even if I was pregnant, something seemed very wrong. While I let my imaginations run amuck with happy visions of Ted's baby, she scheduled an appointment for me with an old German doctor in the nearby town of Lancaster. The term "nearby" is relative when speaking of distances in the desert. Lancaster occupied barren sands over forty miles away.

I lay on the padded table in the brightly lit examining room while Mom sat in one of the two bedside chairs. The doctor's bald head and pudgy face bobbed up and down as he pressed a few different spots on my belly.

"How does this feel?" He pushed firmly on my lower right side. I yelped and nearly jumped off the table. My imagined pregnancy turned out to be appendicitis and he ordered me hospitalized immediately.

With the finesse of a logging man wielding a chain saw, the not-so-delicate German cut a massive crooked roadway from my crotch to my belly button. "Exploratory surgery," he explained later. It turned out my appendix was eight inches long and kinked like a checkmark. My souvenir of the exploration remains to this day a gnarly scar nearly half an inch wide dividing my lower belly into a semblance of a couple of butt cheeks.

After recovery, I was never able to jump on a trampoline again. That would have required a very large diaper. And once in PE, when we were doing gymnastics, the teacher insisted I complete my routine on the parallel bars. At one point in the routine, the lower bar pressed into my abdomen (or rather my abdomen pressed into the bar), and I crumpled onto the floor. She wouldn't budge at the hit to my grade.

In the spring of '69, I had no intention of attending Mojave High School's Junior-Senior Prom. Ted was not there. I faced a dilemma when my name appeared on the list of candidates for Prom Queen, elected by the junior student council. How did that even happen? I had no clue I was popular. I had a couple of girlfriends and, in our small town of California City, everyone hung out together down at the rec center. I did not consider any comparison of my status to the popular girls I had known in San Jose. They were in a completely different league than me. As it turned out, my big city status had been something of an anomaly in the archaic little school in the middle-of-the-desert town of Mojave. I discovered then, there had been a lot of guys wanting to take me out, but I had made it perfectly clear I was unavailable.

Flattered to be nominated, I had to find a date for the prom. I asked a football hero who had graduated the year before. He was more than happy to accompany me.

I wish I could say it was a magical evening. I wish I could say my heart danced when they placed the crown on my head. I wish I could say I enjoyed my date. But I didn't. Being named prom queen boosted my ego, but my football hero practically ignored me before the crown, then grew tentacles after my coronation. After the prom, and midnight breakfast at the local diner, I did not resist when he began kissing me in his truck in front of my house. Then, suddenly his kisses hurt. He forced me down on the truck seat. I fought to escape, but he pinned me to the seat. I finally bit down on his tongue. He snapped back, growling, and grabbed his mouth, releasing me. I burst out of the truck clutching my torn panties, slammed the door, and never looked back.

The ongoing boost to the memory of my ego is my full-page photo in the yearbook … alone.

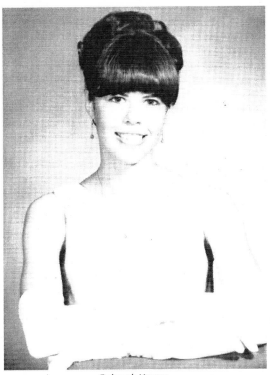

Deborah Hauser

1969
Junior-Senior Prom Queen

Graduation was fast approaching. I ranked in the Top 10 of my class, a rather odd occurrence considering I took an F in chemistry during my junior year rather than fight to make it up after a lengthy illness. I wasn't quite sure whether my ranking was a testament to my good grades, or rather a statement towards the lack of passing grades in our backwoods class of fifty-four seniors. Grades just weren't that important to many of the kids there … except for Band class.

But gloating begets bad karma: I took my driver's test just before one of the graduation practices and looked forward to showing off my license when I arrived at the gymnasium. However, during the test I failed to look over my shoulder when changing lanes. I didn't know you were supposed to look over your shoulder when changing lanes. I had never heard about the legendary blind spot. I didn't even get to show the grouchy examiner how well I could parallel park. As soon as I neglected to look over my shoulder for the lane change, he made me stop, turn around, and go back to the DMV. It was a fail-on-the-spot, hammer-coming-down, immediate reaction … like in Monopoly: "go straight to jail, do not pass go, do not collect $200!" I wished I hadn't told so many people I was taking the test that day.

Summer welcomed me with open arms that year, the beginning of the adventure of the rest of my life. Just after graduation, I wore the crown of Miss California City. I worked at the "Vacation Center," where travelers arrived from all over the country to see and hear the promise of the city of the future. Great Western Cities had invested millions in the venture, and I was the poster girl. I pushed Ted back into the hidden recesses of my mind, accepting dates and dinners and romance from attractive strangers and members of visiting entertainment groups.

A man-made lake backed up to the Vacation Center and, in the evenings, we often took rowboats out to the fake-forest island and made out under the stars. It was exciting and new. Los Angelenos promised me future excursions when I arrived in L.A., having been accepted to the Fashion Merchandising Institute in North Hollywood. The photographer who did the publicity photos for Great Western Cities promised me fame and fortune. After all, he said, he had launched Marilyn Monroe. The VP of Marketing at Great Western Cities corporate offices in Hollywood guaranteed me a part-time job in his office to help work my way through fashion school. My future was a bright and shining star. I would not be poor like my parents.

My mom and dad bought me a Corvair for graduation. More accurately, they obtained the used car with a small down payment, but their lack of income required I make the monthly payments to keep the car. Still, I considered it a terrific gesture. I often drove the car out beyond the city limits into the vast open spaces of the desert. By then, I had acquired a whole new appreciation for its beauty.

One day close to sunset, I drove far off the beaten path. I stopped the car and stood, leaning against it while admiring the magnificence of creation before me. I had started having conversations with the God I knew very little about. I was happy, and I thanked Him for it. Tears even welled up in my eyes. I buried the ugliness of my past sins and looked forward to my successful future. As I gazed thankfully at the approaching sunset, I became aware of the great and awesome silence. Then the great and awesome silence became crushing ... then terrifying. The silence pounded. I couldn't get in my car fast enough. I fumbled with the keys before starting the car. I skidded and threw sand as I stomped on the gas, turning 180 degrees back to the main road.

Breathing a little easier back on the black asphalt, I still kept my speed up, escaping the oppression behind me. Then … WHACK! Feathers and blood splattered up to my windshield; something hit the front of the car. Too frightened to stop, I made my way to the edge of town before pulling over and investigating the mess on the front grill of my Corvair. It had made mincemeat of a poor owl who had flown through the wrong air space at the wrong time. That was the last of my solo adventures to the middle of the intimidating desert to commune with a God I barely knew. Nobody else I knew was talking to him either.

I fled the desolation of the desert, at seventeen years old, for the bright lights of the city, fashion school the key to my future. I grabbed at independence, freedom, and prosperity in Los Angeles. I tasted prime rib in Santa Barbara and Eggs Benedict in Palm Springs. I partied in the Hollywood Hills and danced at the trendy "Candy Store" in Beverly Hills. I shared the pageant stage at the San Bernardino Orange Festival with a couple dozen ravishing women and the Doodletown Pipers. One gentleman I shared a bed with introduced me to the sumptuous pornography of The Marquis de Sade movie.

The allure of riches taunted. Desire embraced darkness and dressed it in gold. It wrapped a noose around my neck, the rope disguised as need … desperate need.

Just after graduation, I wore the crown of Miss California City.

෬   ෬   ෬   ෬   ෬

11 – The Death of Self-Respect

"Never lose yourself while trying to hold on to someone
who doesn't care about losing you."
Lessons Learned in Life

The letter sat in my lap, unopened. It was from Ted. From Viet Nam. I didn't want to open that part of my mind or heart. Like the bright lights in a police interrogation room, just the presence of the letter peeled back a shroud of darkness, revealing my weaknesses and my selfish greed. I did not wear vulnerability well and the knot in my stomach cinched tighter. Ted was coming home on leave. Innocence had taken flight and Ted was on that plane.

We arranged to meet at an Orange County racetrack. He loved cars and the smell of a racetrack. Before he left for Nam, we spent many dates at auto races, especially drag races with acrid fumes filling the air, a constant grin on Ted's gorgeous face. Guilt, far beyond "mixed feelings", swamped my emotions. I couldn't find the "undying" love I had claimed just a year and a half earlier. A lot had happened since our last night together. I did not want to rip open the self-inflicted wounds.

He hadn't changed a bit … but I had. Our awkward evening together ended early. He went back for another tour of duty in Viet Nam and survived another eighteen months as a helicopter door-gunner. I never saw him again.

My roommate Kathy and I were fighting. I came home one day to find all her things gone, except for one dresser. I wanted to escape my present circumstances, move somewhere else, start over. Depression, finances, life in general … *what happened?*

When I moved to Los Angeles, I was full of ambition, confident in my abilities. Now, ugly desire, spurred by my stepfather's depraved proclivities, held me in its clutches. I grabbed at far-too-intimate and, sometimes, dangerous relationships that lasted only days or weeks. The carbon-monoxide poisoning incident with Walt still loomed fresh in my rear-view mirror. Fashion school tuition, living expenses, and payments for my Corvair graduation present still had to be paid. My parents would not, or could not, contribute a dime. Going home to my stepfather was not an option.

I desperately wanted a life free from the darkness that dragged me down. In the midst of the overwhelming struggle, I quit fashion school and went to work full time as the receptionist at the first employment agency I visited. It was a change, but now I aimlessly wandered through my days and stumbled with a sense of failure.

Standing at a bus-stop on my way home from work one sunny Los Angeles day, I noticed a man watching me through the window of his shiny brown mustang. Clean-cut, business-like, and attractive, my eyes met his, which gave him invitation to pull up to the curb.

"Hi, can I give you a ride?" His blue eyes sparkled. A smile curled at the edge of his lips, revealing a row of straight white teeth. The soft curls of his well-trimmed brown hair framed his gently squared face.

Never accept a ride from a stranger. But he was so good looking. And he seemed OK.

"We can go get a bite to eat," he continued. "There's a place just down the street that's pretty good ... plenty of people ... we won't be alone."

I jumped from the frying pan into the fire. "*Beware of the wolf in sheep's clothing!*" *(paraphrased from Matthew 7:15)*

Brian was a dream-come-true, a palliative balm to my troubled soul. We spent nearly every night together, listened to romantic music by Andy Williams, and ate abalone he brought home from his own deep-sea diving. When I became sick with a vicious infection, he nursed me through it with all the kindness of the most benevolent caretaker. Immediately upon my recovery, I rented the available apartment next door to his, and our units became as one.

I loved and felt loved. I imagined the wedding, the gown, our house, and our children. My insecurities were on their way to obscurity.

We slept together. We ate together. We did everything together—for the first three months. Then Brian, while professing his immense love for me, made it clear that marriage was not on the horizon. In fact, he stated, it was important that we both date other people. Our relationship, he proffered, was greatness in the openness we would have to share our love and intimacy with multiple partners.

An emotional vise twisted and turned, crushing me till I choked on my own inadequacy. The first time another woman spent the night at Brian's apartment, nausea welled from my gut, pounded my heart, and burned my throat in an attempt to escape. Midnight passed into morning and sleep refused entrance into this self-made den of lions. Rationalization for this "open relationship", this jagged excuse for love, demanded a scabrous perspective. And I was willing to give it.

Wasted and exhausted, I effused calm and cool on my balcony the next morning. I endured Brian introducing his "date" to me. A less needy person would have ended the relationship, but I held on like a drowning man to a life preserver on the sinking Titanic.

I stood on the edge of an abyss. I spread my wings like a hawk, stepped off the edge and rode the wind currents into the depths of that abyss. The relationship turned into a competition to see who could sleep with more partners ... and I never had been satisfied with second place in any race.

"You are a murderer!" says Sandeep Maheshwari. "After knowing something or someone is devaluing you, still sticking with them is murdering to your self-respect." I might offer an additional viewpoint and say it is the beginning of a long and protracted suicide.

ભ ભ ભ ભ ભ

Brian accompanied me to the prom at the fashion school I had attended. (Technically, I was still enrolled.) While there, one of the teachers approached me with a job referral in the menswear industry, a showroom girl for a well-known company a neighbor of hers owned. She hadn't offered the job to any of the other students because she felt the first time a man "pinched them on the 'derriere'", they would run home crying to Mama. She thought I would be perfect for the job.

The old brick building in downtown Los Angeles housed both production and sales for Kennington Ltd., a prominent men's shirts manufacturer. Excitement and nerves competed for prominence on the day of my interview. I waded through the homeless on the sidewalks and the fanatics raving and waving signs that stated, "Repent. The end is near!"

The showroom, located on the second floor, handsomely carpeted, with racks of shirts on all sides, gave rise to even more giddiness. I wanted this job. My teacher's neighbor, one of the two owners of the company, stepped in, shook my hand, gave me a quick look-over, and asked when I could start. I restrained the excitement bursting from inside while I filled out the necessary paperwork for my immediate employment, the dawn of my career in the fashion industry.

In the 1970's, Kennington was to shirts what Levi was to jeans. My teacher had been correct about her assessment of the attitudes, where the f-word populated each sentence and exclamation from all players in this menswear industry. I fit right in.

With my newly acquired salary, I immediately purchased a brand new, lime green, 1971, Fiat 850 Spider, a convertible with a license plate that read "BEEP." My failing Corvair no longer played a role in my rise to the future. Oh, yes! I had arrived. There was another gal at Kennington, a few years older than me. Judy, with her college education and a few years of experience, took me under her wing and taught me everything I needed to succeed at this company. I learned more in my first week at Kennington than I had learned in my entire six months at the Fashion Merchandising Institute.

I met buyers and sellers and men's department heads from all of the upscale department stores. Kennington's own sales team hailed from all across the country. Kennington owned the license for Mickey Mouse prints on woven shirts, and we sold hundreds-of-thousands of them. Part of my job included traveling to the upscale department stores and taking inventories, then advising the buyers on how many of our shirts they were selling, and how many were needed to stock the racks again. (This was long before the days of computers and digital sales tracking.)

I became Account Executive for the fashionable Bullocks, J.W. Robinsons, and the less fashionable, but larger volume seller, Roos Atkins. I had never been able to shop in any of these stores in all my life. My wardrobe had always been either handmade, hand-me-downs, or plucked from the shelves of a thrift store. Now, I felt like a queen as I strode past the elegant racks, excited to be a part of making the magic happen.

I flew on my first commercial flight while working for Kennington. Terrified and excited at the same time, I reveled in my newly attained value as I ascended the steps to the plane and found my seat. My stomach rose to my throat as the jet engines roared. We hurtled and rumbled down the runway, then whooshed up into the air.

Up in the clouds, I knew I had arrived. I was a somebody and was, indeed, headed for greatness. Not only did the job offer me tremendous career opportunity, it also introduced me to far greater resources in my competition with Brian.

CR   CR   CR   CR   CR

12 – Lessons in the Dark

"Sex is the consolation you have when you can't have love."
Gabriel García Márquez

The door crashed open, a splintering explosion. I saw the uniform and the gun at the same time. My gaze froze on the barrel of the gun pointed at me. My heart thudded. More uniforms. More guns. Terror and confusion swamped the four of us in the candlelit cottage tucked behind my apartment building. The sweet smell of incense shifted bitter at the intrusion. My mind raced to make sense of the present tense.

My friend and neighbor, Jeremy, had returned from a singer-songwriter gig barely thirty minutes earlier. He shared the highlights of his evening with those of us who had stopped by. He pulled a hand-rolled joint from his pocket and offered it around to his guests, all of whom declined.

"Some dude came up to me after my set," he explained. "Said he liked my music, wanted me to partake of this with him. I told him I needed to leave, but then he insisted I take it with me for later. Kept insisting. I finally took it. Didn't want to hurt his feelings. I mean, he did like my music."

Jeremy dropped the unwanted smoke into a small copper bowl on the coffee table. It took up residence with a few other items: a handful of mixed buttons, a couple of paper clips, a cigarette lighter, and a dark incense cone. We all sipped Diet Coke as none of us was old enough to drink alcohol yet, except for my boyfriend Brian, but he hadn't joined me down at Jeremy's. And Jeremy, sweet Jeremy, was a stickler for following rules.

The police officers stormed the room, followed by the undercover detective who had insisted Jeremy take the joint back at the coffee house.

The uniformed officers patted us down and then lead each of us by gunpoint into separate rooms. A burly, gruff-voiced cop directed me into Jeremy's bedroom. I shuddered when he shut the door behind us and commanded me to sit on the bed. It was just him and me and his gun. My head pounded and my vision blurred, his trigger finger my focal point. By the time my vision cleared, he had asked his few questions and then told me I was free to go.

I sat, stunned, shaken, a prisoner suddenly released. I had pleaded Jeremy's innocence, but when I ventured out into the hall, they were jostling him away in handcuffs. Jeremy's head hung, tears on his cheeks. My heart wrenched for this tender young man, working hard to be a musician, but taken down by an over-eager detective needing to flaunt his balls. And the only reason Jeremy even had the joint in the first place was because he didn't want to hurt someone's feelings.

Like a virgin defiled, an angry wall rose up around me, separating me, ripping me from my childhood trust in cops. Another piece of innocence torn away, more muddied waters to navigate … to survive.

I never saw Jeremy again.

ଔ   ଔ   ଔ   ଔ   ଔ

February 9, 1971, in the still dark of the early morning, while sleeping soundly in Brian's bed, the world exploded around us. Violence struck like the hammer of God, threw us from the bed. The silhouetted trees outside our second-story window jerked back and forth, an unrelenting pendulum against the backdrop of fiery explosions. Boom! Boom! Boom! One right after the other, a racing parade ripping down the center of the normally quiet street.

Earthquake! The barrage pounded mercilessly, then stopped. The Sylmar quake, 6.5 on the Richter scale, lasted twelve seconds. Rumblings growled beneath us. The voice of my mother and grandmother echoed from throughout my childhood: "California is just waiting to die." The tidal wave. I knew the tidal wave followed right behind it. I crumbled in the imaginings of the approaching torrential onslaught racing to sweep me into oblivion. The wave never came.

The world around us shook and tumbled, the epicenter only eight miles from our home. As it eased, my adrenalin still pumped to the point I could not stay in bed until the alarm clock rang. Amidst repeating aftershocks and on autopilot, I prepped myself for a day of work. I needed normal. But what could be normal when the ground we walked on would not be still? The exploding gas mains left gaping holes up our street yet I somehow managed to drive my car out and make it into work almost on time, down to the old brick building that still stood. Others came too.

Freeways collapsed that day. The news photos showed a pickup bed jutting out from under an overpass, its cab with driver flattened under the tons of concrete.

The aftershocks continued. Everyone around me put on brave faces, but each time the rumbling began, fear exposed itself in widened eyes and tightened gestures. We went on with our workdays, the homeless still begged, and each of us moved forward in our own lane, because our lane was still unscathed, our paths not blocked. We hid our eyes from the destruction around us so that it wouldn't touch us.

For a month of aftershocks, I lived in masked trepidation. Finally, the earth quieted and my body began to relax. Normal self-effacing fears returned, those fears of need: need to be loved, need to be significant, need to not be alone. Needs requiring self-degradation to achieve the illusion.

Brian was not mine alone, but I loved him. I craved him. I needed him. But there was a space in my needs he refused to fill. I had to prove my value and my desirability ... both to him and to me.

Phil walked into the Kennington offices a few weeks after the earthquake. He stood talking with the receptionist, a friend he had stopped by to see. As I walked past on my way out of the building for my lunch break, our eyes met.

"Debbie," the receptionist spoke up. "This is my friend Phil I was telling you about ... the agent with the Federal Bureau of Narcotics Investigation."

"Guilty," the blond man nodded, his green eyes still locked on mine.

"I'm tied up and can't take a lunch break," Susan said smiling ... and winking. "Why don't you two go to lunch together instead?"

Phil smiled and, in his handsome gray overcoat, gestured towards the door. It was time to plunge headlong into that competition with Brian.

I plunged into the passionate and exhilarating affair. Phil lived and worked out of New York; his partner shot and killed the week before in a drug raid there. There was something thrilling about dabbling on the edge of that danger. He traveled often to Los Angeles and to Mexico for his work but could never share any of the details with me. I received postcards from Mexico City, phone calls from unknown locations, and always visits following a Los Angeles assignment.

Phil fell in love. He wanted to marry me. Living on the edge of that danger was fine; it was acceptable. Opening my heart to a man who could be killed at any moment? … beyond my capabilities. He was a notch on my belt, a marker in a competition. I had played my game well. And I hurt him. I hurt him without guilt. I only wanted the sex, momentary pleasure … revenge. I loved Brian.

"He who hardens his heart will fall into calamity," the Bible warns. My heart was hardening out of necessity for survival. Determined to go down this road, I descended into deeper darkness, into calamity.

I enjoyed parties with tall and lanky Horst, chef and chauffer to a famous Hungarian Hollywood actress. Gymnastic gyrations in the front seat of his sportscar were interrupted by pleading marriage proposals. "You need someone to take care of you," he repeated over and over until my only exit strategy involved shattering his heart.

I met Meinrod, a reserved businessman from Switzerland, at Alpine Village, a wonderful German marketplace/village with a restaurant and a dance floor where I loved to whirl round and round dancing the polka. Meinrod was much too reserved to dance the polka. I encountered him outside the shops. Tall, husky, business suit, overcoat … his smoldering eyes peered out from under his hat. He watched me as I entered the restaurant. When I left, I saw him again outside another shop, his smoldering eyes still watching me. Those eyes begged introduction and I dove in.

After many nights in my bed, tender loving nights, he visited my stepfather and asked for my hand in marriage. I refused to move to Switzerland, to another culture, to a male-dominated culture with a language different than mine. The tender loving nights ended. Brian comforted me at the loss.

Like movie reviews, Brian and I shared the details of our exploits, comforted each other at the losses. We were soulmates living in darkness. In his search to find meaning in our darkness and still hold onto that darkness, Brian became entranced by a spiritualist and author, Edgar Cayce, and drew me into his quest.

Edgar Cayce, in his books, wrote that he read the Bible through every year. In my miniscule exposure to Christianity, I accepted Cayce's words as truth because, after all, in my mind the Bible was good ... though I would not read it for myself. It represented good so Edgar Cayce must be good. We were a product of our many lives, our reincarnations, he said. Me and Brian, soulmates. As Cayce said:

"A soulmate is an ongoing connection with another individual that the soul picks up again in various times and places over lifetimes. We are attracted to another person at a soul level not because that person is our unique complement, but because by being with that individual, we are somehow provided with an impetus to become whole ourselves."

Inside, I craved that wholeness. Together, we continued plummeting through darkness, clinging to every justification, to every perversion.

છ છ છ છ છ

13 – The Playboy Mansion

"It is beautiful, it is endless, it is full and yet seems empty. It hurts us."
Jackson Pearce, Fathomless

Brian continued to tell me I was beautiful. "Beautiful and inspiring," he said. "Bill Figge, a well-known photographer for Playboy Magazine has his studio right here in Glendale," he told me.

Flattered, yet hesitant, I wanted to do anything he asked. He made the call. He scheduled the screen test. And suddenly there I was … naked, in front of the camera lens of the famous Bill Figge.

I felt naked, very naked. I was naked! My nerves, with the weight of an anvil, crushed my chest. NOTHING was hidden, not even that ugly "appendectomy surgery" scar. Mr. Figge wasn't concerned about the scar, nor did he seem concerned about the fact that I was completely naked right there in front of him. Perhaps it was that overwhelming lack of concern that finally put me at ease. He respected me. He saw me only through the lens, the finished photograph in his mind … his artwork. His wife scurried around as his assistant, adjusting lights, adjusting my hair, observing the sculpture-in-progress that was me.

After a successful screen test, Mr. Figge, along with his wife, began plans for a centerfold layout. We set up in the fashionable interior of the home of a gay friend of Brian's, a hairdresser with a uniquely decorated private salon in his Hollywood Hills home: rustic grape-stake fencing on walls mixed with gilded antiques in an amber gas-lamp glow. Art Deco met the Victorian Age, along with Botticelli and Gustav Klimt accents. And Debbie Hauser reclined naked in the antique barber's chair, my long brown hair glistening in the filtered light.

I loved every minute of the exhausting all-day photo shoot. I did not feel exploited in any way. I loved the camera and it loved me. Fantasies of modeling swirled in my head. I wanted to do this every day for a career, clothes or no clothes. It didn't matter. I could do anything, as long as it was in front of the camera.

The resulting photos were stunning. Mr. Figge submitted them to the West Coast editor for Playboy Magazine. She invited me for an interview. Her harsh objectivity reflected her business perspective on my future as a Playboy Centerfold. My bottom teeth were crooked, she pointed out. A gift from my biological father and then my poor parents who could not afford the cost of braces. She told me about a handy little veneer I could have made, that would slip in and out, as needed, to disguise my very jagged lower bite, kind of a snap-in smile. I immediately followed her advice. She approved my photos for publication, but that was just step one in the journey of the photos to a centerfold spread.

Next, the entire staff of twelve editors in Chicago liked my photos and passed them on to the big guy himself, Hugh Heffner. But Hugh Heffner had a problem with gracing a centerfold with my image. Pictures of me, he said, looked too much like pictures of his then girlfriend, Barbi Benton. He dashed my centerfold dreams.

Looking back in hindsight, I think God himself was honoring that six-year-old little girl's commitment to him so many years earlier. If I had been accepted, I would have been contracted to Playboy for five years, and who knows where that life may have taken me. (Although, I made enough of a mess myself, even without the Playboy umbrella.) The blow softened immensely when I received the coveted invitation to Hugh Hefner's housewarming party for his Holmby Hills mansion.

CR   CR   CR   CR   CR

10236 Charing Cross Road. My nerves sizzled. Stress-induced tunnel vision prevented the building of encompassing visual memories. I handed my invitation to the attendant, aware only of the shrubbery behind him and glittering lights in the darkness. My car entered the wonderland. Then I stood inside the fairytale castle. Dazed. Confused. Awed.

Another girl, about my age, recognized a sister fish-out-of-water. "Would it be okay if we hang out together?" she asked.

I melted with relief, realized I wasn't breathing, and let the air rush in. Temporary insanity ran like rivulets down my consciousness, making space for a smile and semi-rational thought.

We wove our way through the milling crowds of beautiful people. Two more beautiful people: my companion, scheduled for centerfold publication a few months hence; me, hardly feeling the sting of my own rejection, still one of the beautiful people.

Lights and music drew us outside the back of the house. Tables, laden with exotic foods and ice sculptures, stretched over the finely clipped lawns. A couple of older guys engaged us in conversation and brought us cocktails. Charming and classy, they led us through the 12-bedroom mansion, out through the front door, and into another wing of the sprawling stone digs.

"Servants quarters," they said. Charming and classy devolved into slick and menacing. Miss Maybe-November and I found excuse to slip back into the mansion proper.

Then I saw them. Hugh Hefner and Barbi Benton. She stood on the lower steps of the rounded staircase. He stood on the marble floor basking in his role of host.

Short! My first thoughts stumbled. They were both much shorter than I expected. Reality diminishes giants. In my wedge heels, my eyes were level with his. And Barbi? In person, I didn't resemble her at all. She was tiny and petite ... my 5'7" frame, a staggering oaf next to her.

That's the last I remembered of my consolation prize. I didn't recognize any of the famous movie stars in person. I read about them the next morning in the newspaper. I had rubbed shoulders with many mega stars of 1971.

The experience bordered on surreal. It built my sense of value, but I did not belong in those surroundings. Occasionally I conjure up memories of the wide and curving stairway, or see the tables piled with food, outdoors, among the ice sculptures. But I'm not sad at the loss. I am grateful I was protected from a journey down a dangerous, self-serving, superficial road. Ironically, at the time, I justified it as preservation of my self-respect.

My not-so-dream-come-true Brian was happy to have one of the Playboy nude photos of me framed as a large portrait on his bedroom wall in our quiet neighborhood of Glendale.

○③　○③　○③　○③　○③

14 – Hot Pants and Hot Men

"Regardless of what society says, we can't go on much longer in the sea of immorality without judgment coming."
Billy Graham

There are some people who wear their authority with confidence, their power with assurance. There are some people who just know they are of value to the world around them and behave in that knowledge. I am not one of those people. I was, however, sitting at a table full of those people, enjoying a fancy evening at a fancy restaurant in Palm Springs.

It was my first Menswear Show. In those days, it happened every October in Palm Springs and every spring in San Diego. Buyers and sellers from across the country gathered together in a spirit of great pomp and celebration to introduce their new season of fashions and determine what men would be buying at every retail outlet in the months hence.

I had been invited to join this group of heavy hitters in the industry for dinner that night. I was one of the beautiful people. Well, I may have looked beautiful but that was truly as far as it went. My attempts at mimicking confidence hovered at absurd in my mind but generally I managed the charade. My dinner order of prime rib and baked potato arrived. I grabbed the white cup of sour cream from the plate and heaped all of it onto my perfectly baked potato. I smushed and smashed it all in with butter and salt. Then, with great anticipation, I plunged a sizeable forkful into my mouth. Time stopped. My brain whipped around in an immediate effort to minimize impending disaster. My eyes began to water, and my throat closed. That was NOT sour cream. It was horseradish!

Smile. Smile. Smile.

Don't gag. Don't gag. Don't gag.

Nice heavy linen napkin on lap. Nice heavy linen napkin in hand. Casually, nonchalantly, wipe mouth … smile … horseradish gone. No potato with dinner tonight.

And thus began my journey with self-importance.

Aside from the horseradish, I loved Palm Springs. I adapted quickly to the party that lasted for days. Kennington was big enough that we occupied an entire motel on the main street. The swimming pool was ours … 24/7. Our sales team gathered from across the country and, boy, did we put that pool to use for much adult activity that eventually spilled from the pool and into private rooms. We worked hard during the day and we played hard all night. With very few notable exceptions, one's marital status had no standing in Palm Springs. Palm Springs became my playground every October, a hotbed of promiscuity. Many beautiful and not-so-beautiful players, many willing participants.

Looking back, I have to respect and admire our Sales Manager at the time, and I must mention it here lest his reputation be sullied by my previous words. There were very few men I could not entice into bed. He was the most solid of those few. And, believe me, I gave it every possible shot.

Back in the 1970's, "hot pants" emerged as a hot fashion item for women. Denim short-shorts became the new skirt. We wore them with knee-high boots and big hair. I flaunted them well. The menswear industry jumped into the fray and when those players visited the Kennington offices, they always brought plenty of samples to me personally.

When Kennington introduced Kennington for Gals, they made me their fitting model, the perfect size 9 from which all their other sizes were cut. When Kennington introduced the tattoo shirt at one of the San Diego shows, my role as showroom girl included donning a hot pink bikini with my exposed body covered in temporary tattoos.

Each year in Palm Springs, Kennington hosted the industry-wide party of the year on the Saturday night. Levi threw theirs on Sunday. Big budgets funded these soirees and I thrived in the excitement and the attention. When I designed a daring and revealing gown for one of our Palm Springs parties, our manufacturing manager was happy to create the pattern and make me the red-carpet-newsworthy dress.

For one Palm Springs event, a visually delectable actor appeared in Kennington's short-movie promotion of that fall's fashion introductions. My primary day job at that show involved presenting the brief film to hundreds of buyers throughout the day. When the actor himself walked into the darkened room the afternoon of the first day, I may have actually drooled. He happily accepted my invitation to the Kennington party that Saturday night ... and my invitation to my hotel room for an after-party ... and many nights thereafter back in Los Angeles. Back in Los Angeles, I also accepted his invitation to the smaller parties of multiple and interchangeable intimate partners ... partners that included other visually delectable movie stars of those early 70's.

The slope was slippery, the downhill slide like a hurtling luge in the Olympics. I rode it hard, my self-worth inflated. I chose desirability, desired by the beautiful people. But it was never enough. We all grabbed for more and more, each one wanting something different yet willing to grab at every degradation to satisfy something deep in our guts. It was a world without God, and we dared not let God in to expose our sin.

℞   ℞   ℞   ℞   ℞

The appeal of Brian was diminishing. Each victory in my competition increased my self-importance while at the same time slicing deeper into any illusion of a moral foundation. Brian saw this. He sensed me slipping.

"Let's buy a house together," he suggested. "We can find one with bedrooms at separate ends of the house so we can each still have our own dates."

We toyed with the possibilities, bantered about our options. But the door he had opened for our outside relationships had unleashed a self-absorbed conquering survivor and warrior in me. The conquest was real. No longer the victim, I needed dominance, I needed control. A shared living space created shackles. I would have married him in a heartbeat, but that was not the offer on the table. I chose instead to increase my freedom, to assert my battle cry. I moved twenty miles away to Granada Hills, a thirty-minute drive from Brian. He was still a confidante, still a partner, still a hope for a permanent relationship. But it was a fracturing hope.

My new home became my own personal brothel, a spacious, two-bedroom den of iniquity. I decorated my "sleeping" room with a combination of the grape-stake fencing I discovered at my Playboy photo shoot, and plenty of gold-veined mirrors. The second "bedroom" was larger with a substantial wet bar. An accomplished artist, I designed and began painting a mural for the long wall in that playroom: a variety of jungle animals in a jungle setting, all in the act of copulation. I was also well known by this time for the pornographic party cakes I decorated. For my twenty-first birthday party, I featured a fountain for the beverages, a statue of a little boy peeing alcoholic concoctions into a punch bowl. Crowds milled through my playhouse; music echoed off the walls.

I sank to unthinkable depths. The men came and went as through a revolving door ... until one night. It was another one-night stand, a large, black man I had picked up at a club like selecting an animal from a cage. Strangers had become my preferred companions. I clawed at my addiction but could not let anyone close. We made rough and passionate use of my mirrored bedroom. Then he slipped out to the kitchen in search of additional refreshments. The refrigerator door opened. A cupboard door opened and closed. A couple of drawers opened and closed. Utensils rattled. But he did not return to the bedroom.

My imaginations awakened to the more sinister possibilities. *Maybe he's looking for a knife, a butcher knife. Maybe he's coming back to stab me, to murder me. I have no clue who this man is. I'm not even sure I remember his name.* No more the conquering victor, the blood drained from my head. My stomach tightened into knots. Paralyzed with fear, I had no one to blame but myself. There was no escape, no exit except to get past him to the front door. Now I was the animal. I was the prey.

He returned to the bedroom, two drinks in hand, ready for more time below the gold-veined mirrors. He was not the murderer. But by now I had nearly murdered any remnants of me.

Daylight was sobering. I couldn't stay in Granada Hills. I couldn't stay in my whore house. Brian was going through some changes too. His conversations included the name Jesus here and there in scattered conversations. He had visited a church. He was searching for something more. How dare he! He's the one who opened this door for me, and now he wants to bring God into the equation? I would have none of it.

I moved to a quiet garden bungalow apartment in Pasadena, a retreat surrounded by ferns and tropical shrubs. Glass walls brought the outdoors in, nature a soothing compress. I travelled out of town for Kennington more and more now. I flew to San Francisco often to manage the Roos Atkins account there. I fell in love with San Francisco and requested a transfer there, a move away in hopes of another restart in my life. But there was not yet enough business there to warrant the expense.

I threw one of my last parties in my Pasadena apartment. A much quieter evening than the boisterous events in Granada Hills. However, I had to leave early the next morning on a flight north and left my house without cleaning up any of the food mess. When I arrived home, tired and exhausted, I opened the front door, hoping to step into my retreat. I knew I had left a mess and was prepared for that. I was not prepared for the six-inch wide highway of ants traversing from the front door, across the hardwood parquet floor of my living room, into the kitchen, up the cabinets, and into the deep fryer still filled with rancid grease. Before I even took off my jacket, I put on my gloves, picked up the fryer, made my way quickly to the dumpster and dropped the entire appliance with all its little passengers into the big metal bin.

ଔ   ଔ   ଔ   ଔ   ଔ

October 1973. I had been at Kennington about four-and-a-half years. I sat with the sales team in a large conference room at the Menswear show in Palm Springs. The conversations focused on increasing sales, new fashion directions, and each of our roles in those objectives. The news had just broken about Egypt and Syria attacking Israel on the Jewish holiday of Yom Kippur. The world was exploding around us and we were sitting in this well-lit, quiet room discussing wealth and fashion.

My mind wandered from the business at hand. *What am I doing here? I need to do something different. I need to be doing something honorable.*

I needed a bigger change than a move to Pasadena. I don't even remember what happened for the rest of the show. I don't remember packing up my apartment in Pasadena. I don't even remember quitting my job. But I did. I left it. I left Brian. I left it all.

ℭ℞ ℭ℞ ℭ℞ ℭ℞ ℭ℞

15 – Search for Significance ... Again

"If you put a small value on yourself, rest assured that the world will not raise your price."
Unknown

There is a haunting beauty to San Francisco. I stood on the balcony of Kyle's apartment atop Twin Peaks, a witness to the spectacle. The fog swirled in the depths below revealing golden glimpses wherever it parted as the sun bid its last adieus to the end of another busy day. The wisps of clouds thickened as they rolled like ocean waves pushing up the sides of the lush green Twin Peaks. They silenced the chaos below and brandished the grandeur of creation in the fading glow of the melting sun through deep white blankets. Then all stood still and quiet in the gathering gray.

I had been on a business trip to San Francisco when I first witnessed this end-of-day splendor. I hadn't finished all my necessary paperwork, so I needed to reschedule my flight home. Kyle, one of the buyers for Roos Atkins, invited me to stay in his apartment, since he was heading away for the weekend. On my way into the building, key in hand, I passed a handsome stranger at the mailboxes. Engaging green eyes smiled from his olive-toned face, caught my attention. I continued to turn my head as

I passed, returning his smile. From the staircase a floor above his, I watched his dark head enter the end apartment and felt a strange camaraderie as we shared a proximity of space in this building above "The City."

Evening darkness invaded Kyle's apartment. I flipped on the lights over his boxy, square dining table and spread my work out across its shiny surface. I dug for a pencil in my briefcase, flustered that I couldn't find a single one. I guiltily rifled through Kyle's drawers hoping to find that needed pencil. Nothing.

"Well," I spoke out loud to myself, "I did kind of meet that guy downstairs. I know we didn't talk," I continued my argument, "but our eyes met ... and that's good enough for me." I scurried down the stairs and knocked on his door.

After I finished my paperwork that evening, thanks to the borrowed pencil, Matteo had invited me down for a glass of wine. The evening ended with this sensitive, fascinating man giving me a sumptuous foot massage. His engaging green eyes looked deep into my soul ... and he didn't know about my reputation in Los Angeles.

Occasional phone calls followed. When it came time to leave everything behind in southern California, Matteo's door was open wide, and I moved in with him atop Twin Peaks.

CR CR CR CR CR

I reclined on the comfy beanbag in the late morning sunlight. Classical Bach filled the air from the National Public Radio broadcast. Matteo served me quiche and hot tea. A typical Sunday morning in San Francisco. Later in the day, we would stroll Polk Street down in the heart of the city, dine at an eclectic vegetarian restaurant, and likely take in another foreign film.

Matteo was a vegetarian, immensely focused on his health. So I became a vegetarian. Matteo loved classical music. That was not a stretch for me. I enjoyed the ambiance of it though I could not name each composer and etude as he did. He coddled his record player like a delicate sculpture, each vinyl 33 carefully wiped and protected as fine pieces of art. Boston ferns, spider plants, dieffenbachias, and more flourished and filled his apartment under his auspicious care. He called them each by their botanical names. With all of that serenity as backdrop, it was hard to picture him in his business brilliance while he worked as a contracts administrator with the Small Business Administration. Suit, tie, and briefcase in hand every day, after his run and protein smoothie, he drove his Porsche 914, white body, black top, down the hill to the stoic grey government buildings of his employment.

For my own work in the city, I started working as a free-lance merchandising consultant with a sales rep contact from my "old life." Additionally, through a contact from my fashion school days, I connected with the Fashion Institute of California (FIC) in San Francisco. For the FIC, I traveled throughout the Bay Area in then-current fashionable attire, hat required, and heels, and lectured at Career Days in high schools about careers in the fashion industry. I loved showing the kids the whole world I had discovered in the fashion industry that I had never known existed until my days on the Teen Fashion Boards. I enjoyed their curiosity, their questions I had answers for, their motivation, and their desire to emulate me. Of course, it was only the me I revealed to them. No one in Northern California knew the cavernous depths of my previous life.

I also enrolled in the Grimmé modeling school at the famous Grimmé Modeling Agency in San Francisco. Taught by a gorgeous tall model who had a current television commercial running, I learned the details about photo makeup, working with the camera, the grueling photo shoots ... and, like the Playboy photo shoot, I loved every minute of it. My 5'7" frame needed to weigh in at 118 pounds. But the owner of the agency said I was fine at 123; I carried my weight well. I was accepted by the agency and my first paid photo shoot featured a line of turquoise jewelry on a semi-nude assignment. I was willing to work nude or semi-nude which, in those days, payed double at $100 an hour. I worked a couple more similar jobs before my inner tumult began seeping back in.

Photo shoots at the Grimmé Modeling Agency.

I turned to food. I missed eating red, juicy steaks when I was with Matteo, so I over-indulged in vegetarian goodies. Cakes, cookies, pies, and candy bars all qualify under the vegetarian umbrella. Matteo was good to me, life was good, but there was a piece missing. I didn't know what it was. I filled it with food. The photographers were not interested in plumper models those days, so Grimmé no longer sent me out on profitable jobs. The owner said I could be great, go to Los Angeles, New York, fashion capitals of the world … if I could keep my weight down. My emotional demons clawed through my desire to succeed. Matteo was not especially appreciative of the extra pounds I had acquired, but it wasn't grounds for breaking up, just the trigger for a little less intimacy.

Matteo was entranced with the occult and metaphysics. However, his definition of occult varied from what I originally understood to be connotations of evil and Satanic. Rather Matteo spoke of white witches vs black witches, like day and night, good and evil. He studied the writings of Helen Blavatsky, a Russian occultist, philosopher and author who co-founded the Theosophical Society in the late 1800's. Theosophy, she defined as the synthesis of science, religion, and philosophy—a reviving of an ancient wisdom. She was one of the early persons who influenced the rise of the New Age Movement.

Matteo introduced me to his friend and mentor, Dr. Robert Leichtman. We spent many evenings in his home in Sausalito. He was something of a psychic, diagnosed illnesses of people in completely different parts of the country—not by seeing them but through spirit guides. The most significant skill of Dr. Leichtman was his ability to do life readings, that is to explore previous lives that people lived in their journey to this life. In my life reading, he told me I had lived on a southern plantation back in the days of the Civil War. It was especially intriguing to me as I found out years later that my ancestors had actually owned a plantation and slaves in the old South. Today I have my own thoughts and ideas on the matter of life readings and reincarnation, especially in view of the fact he said he was never able to do a life reading on a Christian. But that is a discussion for another time and another place. Suffice it to say, that when he could not read a Christian, it planted another dark arrow of fear in my heart.

I shoved aside the fears and doubts. I continued to push away a God who saw my sins. It was less convicting to embrace good witches and see everyone as spiritual beings with access to the supernatural, even though I knew the Bible warned to have nothing to do with it. After all, I had my own experiences dabbling in the supernatural and, while smoking pot, great doors of creativity opened deep in my psyche for me. And without God, my sins were not sins.

ଊ   ଊ   ଊ   ଊ   ଊ

I secured a job as a receptionist and administrative assistant at a business furniture design studio in the heart of the downtown warehouse district, just south of the financial district. The owner, Stephanos, a wealthy Greek nearly 30 years my senior, frequently encouraged me to break up with my boyfriend and go out with him instead.

"Well," he finally said after another unsuccessful attempt. "Let me know if you ever do break up with him."

I grew frustrated with my lack of direction. I had left Kennington to pursue a more honorable career. My job at Business Furniture and Design was not it. Neither was the pursuit of modeling, which my inner demons crushed anyway.

Matteo grew depressed with the lack of sunshine in San Francisco proper. We would bundle up in coats in the middle of June, then cross the Golden Gate Bridge for sunshine and beach wear.

We left Twin Peaks and rented a cozy, sunshine-flooded cottage on a quiet street in San Rafael, about a 40-minute drive north of San Francisco in minimal traffic. Matteo commuted to his government job in the city every day, not in minimal traffic. I quit work and enrolled at Marin College to pursue a career in occupational therapy.

For my first stop on that quest, I volunteered at Kent State Hospital, not far from Marin College. They assigned me to the nursery. I stumbled and blundered, completely ignorant about how to care for baby vegetables—I'm sorry, but that is the term that inconsiderate people usually use to describe a person with no conscious activity. I was one of those inconsiderate people. I became frustrated and discouraged with no spirited and loving mentor to encourage me on.

When the director of the hospital heard that I had been a model and worked in the fashion industry, she asked me if I could teach a class in fashion and makeup to the teenage resident-patients there. I quickly agreed.

There were six to eight girls on a regular basis each week. They loved the class. They loved the makeup. They loved dressing in hats and scarves and getting their pictures taken. I fell in love with the girls, but I was challenged. The pimpled uncared-for faces, the drooling mouths, the greasy, stringy hair … I just wasn't prepared. I didn't know how.

I brought tremendous enthusiasm to the class. The girls loved me. Others said, "Oh, you're doing such a wonderful thing!" They didn't know my secrets. They didn't know my inner thoughts. They didn't know my revulsions. I kept at it though, committed to the few-month program.

One of the girls, seventeen-year-old Shirley, was a thalidomide baby from the 50's. She had no arms nor legs, just a stump of a body with feet she used to steer and power her electric wheelchair. She took art classes at Marin College. For Halloween I gave her a gift of sparkle nail polish that she delightedly and immediately requested I apply to her toenails. And for the Halloween party, she wanted to dress up as a pumpkin.

"That's terrible. You can't let her do that!" complained one of the administrators.

"She knows her body type," I argued. "And she's excited about it."

Shirley attended the party as a pumpkin with her sparkle toe-nail polish.

I attended two semesters at Marin College. I excelled at art, English, and French. But I had to admit, I was not cut out for an "honorable" career. I was not cut out to be an occupational therapist. I was not cut out, at that time in my life, as a selfish, self-centered, emotionally stunted human being, to work with the disabled and un-beautiful people. I caught glimpses of their souls and their souls were beautiful. My soul was ugly and did not belong with them.

ଓ   ଓ   ଓ   ଓ   ଓ

I sought out and landed a job in the merchandising offices for a chain of very trendy, discount, labels-removed, women's clothing stores. At the time I hired on at their corporate offices in Menlo Park, they owned thirty-five stores throughout California and were launching a multi-state expansion. It was a ground-floor opportunity with tremendous career potential. I intended to take maximum advantage of that career potential.

At the same time, Matteo finally popped his cork over government bureaucracy. With that bottle completely broken, he accepted a job as a contracts negotiator in the more reasonable, rational, and logical private sector.

Both of our jobs located in the south-bay cities begged shorter commute times. We traded our peaceful San Rafael cottage for a spacious tree-shrouded apartment in Los Gatos. However, it wasn't long after establishing as our favorite restaurant, The Broken Egg in old town Los Gatos, that we had to admit we hadn't shortened our commutes at all. The lack of a lease allowed us to relocate quickly to a garden bungalow duplex in Menlo Park, near both of our jobs. I lived close enough to my job that I occasionally rode my bicycle to work. Peace and sanity settled in.

I loved Matteo. I wanted to marry him and have his babies. But he was unwilling to take that step. For him, he said, the responsibility of a child was far too awesome. I wanted a commitment from him, and he was unwilling to give it.

I grew restless. In view of my crumbling relationship with Matteo, my boss became more physically attractive to me every day. One evening after work, several of my work associates gathered in a hotel lounge for drinks. Too drunk to drive home. I phoned Matteo to tell him I would stay at the hotel that night, and then allowed my boss to help me to a room. Three years of monogamy ended that night.

໒ຊ   ໒ຊ   ໒ຊ   ໒ຊ   ໒ຊ

Matteo and me.

ઉ૪   ઉ૪   ઉ૪   ઉ૪   ઉ૪

16 – The Appeal of Riches

"You can't defeat the demons you enjoy playing with."
Unknown

Perched on one of the many leather-padded bar stools surrounding the large horseshoe-shaped bar, I casually pulled one of the slender brown Virginia Slim cigarettes from the pack in my purse. I glanced around at the several work associates gathered there, as we often were in the after-work hours. Everyone chatted together, drinks in hand, not paying any attention to my current actions. I fingered the cigarette's slim fragrant form. I had smoked pot often over the last few years, but I'd only picked up cigarettes about a week earlier, just a short time after I moved out of the now-Matteo's garden bungalow.

Fashionably dressed in a sleek black pantsuit, I crossed my legs, lit the trendy brown cigarette, and attempted disdainful nonchalance as I slowly inhaled—and exhaled—a brief puff. After a couple more puffs, a warm breath danced across the back of my neck. As I turned, the lips of our rugged warehouse manager nibbled my ear.

He whispered, "Do you know how ridiculous you look smoking that cigarette?"

Without looking at him, I snubbed the cigarette out in the nearby ash tray. It was the last cigarette I ever smoked.

That night I sprawled across my bed and stared at my white ceiling with its old tarnished metal chandelier. I lived in a large Spanish adobe home with a traditional red tile roof, a pottery-tiled floor, a big outdoor space with lots of old large oak trees, and with five other people. It was a grand house, designed for parties and, oh, did we party! Yet it provided each of us privacy in our own secluded bedrooms. There were always new faces around the breakfast table with a rotating bevy of overnight guests, each of us enjoying that privacy of our own secluded bedrooms.

It was time to call Stephanos, my old boss, the wealthy Greek businessman who wanted to be notified if I ever broke up with my boyfriend. And, well, I certainly had broken up with Matteo.

Our first date, I wore my gray ribbon dress, a single narrow gray ribbon swirled round and round, stitched in an elegant design, like a crochet, until it formed a single and complete dress. It was a hand-me-down, though I had been assured it cost a fortune. It looked and felt like a fortune. We drove in his Lincoln Continental to Ondine's in Sausalito. We dined on exquisite fare: quenelles for appetizers, stuffed squab in cherry sauce, asparagus with hollandaise sauce, a Grand Marnier dessert soufflé ... I thought I'd died and gone to heaven. I had never tasted food so good.

For the next two months, I happily accepted the role of Stephanos' arm candy. We spent every weekend together. He kept his Lincoln Continental at his luxury San Francisco apartment and his Maserati at his apartment in Marina Del Rey in southern California. He sailed his yacht out of the San Francisco harbor; his friend sailed a yacht out of Marina Del

Rey. We dined at all the finest restaurants in San Francisco, Los Angeles, and Honolulu, where all of the maître d's greeted him personally.

"Oh, Monsieur Themelaros," in their French accents, "How are you this evening?" We were seated at the best tables.

I enjoyed duckling a l'orange, beef wellington, and always red wine with chocolate mousse for dessert. I left work on Friday afternoons to meet him in the city, then off to our favorite destinations. I arrived at work on Monday mornings, flaunting all the gifts he had purchased for me over that previous weekend. He bought a house in Tiburon and wanted me to make all the design decisions. We planned a trip to Greece for the following Easter. Matteo drifted further and further away from my memories.

On a sunny October afternoon off the coast of Southern California, I lounged with about half a dozen "beautiful people" I didn't know, except for Stephanos and his friend I had just met. We downed plenty of cocktails on the deck of the yacht, land nowhere in sight. One of the guys suddenly stood up and suggested a swim. With that, he dove off the side of the boat. We all laughed and crowded the side from where he had jumped.

"Come on in," he shouted and waved. "It's great."

I peeled off my gauzy dress, revealing my bikini underneath, and plunged into the shimmering blue Pacific Ocean. Nearly everyone followed. We were laughing and splashing when it suddenly occurred to me, *Whoa! It's a long way down there to the bottom … and I have no idea what is swimming below me!* Visions of sharks, octopus, and sting rays filled my imaginations.

Like with my fear of heights, I grew dizzy and frightened. Panic seized me but I struggled to maintain my composure in front of these "beautiful people." I couldn't get to the boat's ladder fast enough. I didn't leave the deck again. Later as we were headed back to shore, heavy fog rolled in, laying like a thick blanket on the now gray waters. Dread wrapped its tentacles around me, but I continued consoling my runaway thoughts. *This man is an experienced yachtsman. No one else seems concerned. I'm sure he knows what he's doing.* We made it to the docks, slowly and safely. But by then I'd pretty much had my fill of sailing on the open ocean.

I loved the Greek restaurants Stephanos shared with me. The food, the dancing, the Ouzo! So, for Thanksgiving, he promised to take me to his favorite Greek restaurant in Honolulu. I had never been to Hawaii and never even had the desire to go … until I was actually there. Wow! The warmth, the blue water, the white sandy beaches … I waded out into the clear waters, so far from shore, yet still wading. I could still see my feet. After the yacht-ocean swimming experience, the visual of my feet was extremely comforting and necessary.

Thanksgiving Day we strode into his favorite Greek restaurant, eager to enjoy an authentic Greek dinner. But, horror of horrors, his favorite Greek restaurant was serving an authentic AMERICAN Thanksgiving dinner with turkey and dressing. Psychological or emotional thwartings are devastating for me. Knocked completely off kilter, I could not find it in me to "enjoy" our authentic American Thanksgiving meal. And thus began my downhill slide in this beautiful island paradise.

The next day as we strolled the streets of Honolulu, I suggested we step into the McDonalds fast food restaurant we passed. At this point I craved an authentic American McDonalds Quarter-Pounder with Cheese.

"No woman of mine will ever eat in a place like that," Stephanos growled. He pulled me in the opposite direction into a lovely outdoor dining restaurant serving a more sophisticated palette. Though I joined him for the perfectly divine meal, my jaw stubbornly set and most conversation ceased.

This man is too controlling! I decided.

Back in the hotel room, without a word to Stephanos, I booked myself a flight for the very next morning rather than stay till Sunday as planned. He followed suit and booked his own seat on the same 747 to California, his seat far from mine.

We landed in SFO. He drove me to his warehouse where my lime-green Fiat with the license plate "BEEP" was parked. I drove off without looking back, out of his life forever.

CR CR CR CR CR

I had tasted of the good life with Stephanos and with many fleeting partners who showered me with gifts and dinners and offers of more. I had sworn, years ago, that I would not be trapped in the poverty I had grown up with. I sought out men from among the "beautiful people." Proposals of marriage had come and gone. Yet there were none I could imagine spending the rest of my life with. In my heart was a deep hole that no one had been able to fill. My desperate need to be loved tore at the gut of my lusts, an agonizing thirst I could not quench. It struggled hand in hand with the need to control my own destiny.

My independence secured once again, I had to face the conflicts arising in my household of six people, in the sprawling adobe known for its parties. Running away was the easiest option. Matteo, now dating someone else, planned to leave our garden bungalow in Menlo Park. I eagerly jumped at the opportunity to re-take possession of this oasis in the bustle of life. It's fern-covered patio, kitchen skylight, and hardwood floors beckoned. Matteo even left the waterbed and the large dieffenbachia plant for me.

My position at work had grown immensely. With 165 stores now throughout the western United States, management discovered they didn't understand the out-of-state markets as well as they anticipated. They set me loose, for an entire year, to travel to each store in each state numerous times. I needed to understand the markets, the clientele, and any other influences on store sales. It was a dream job. I loved it. And I was very good at it.

ଔ   ଔ   ଔ   ଔ   ଔ

7 – Final Descent

"What is hell? Hell is oneself. Hell is alone, the other figures in it merely projections. There is nothing to escape from and nothing to escape to. One is always alone."
T.S. Elliot

My life became a routine of different states or cities every week. Portland, Oregon. Seattle, Washington. (That was my favorite.) El Paso, Texas. Phoenix, Arizona. Las Vegas, Nevada. Salt Lake City, Utah. (I got in a small fender-bender there.) Denver, Colorado, and Colorado Springs. (I nearly got caught in a blizzard there). Check in at the corporate offices on Monday mornings, catch a flight out Monday afternoon, return through SFO Friday nights in time to party all weekend. I thrived in the demanding schedule. I strode in the confidence of my perceived value.

Other women I knew, who traveled for their jobs, usually confined themselves to small restaurants in their small motels. Not me. I had the expense account, and they did as well, but I made maximum use of mine. I enjoyed the nicer restaurants, I met people, I visited the bars. District managers were happy to take me to the best local venues. And I sought out different men every trip in every city.

One evening in Salt Lake City, I sat in the lounge after dinner enjoying wine and the very handsome entertainer. From the stage, his eyes met mine. Certain where the evening was headed, I smiled as he sent a bottle of wine over to my table. Unfortunately, that was the last thing I remembered.

I woke up very groggy. My head felt heavy and, although I knew it was morning by the shaft of light invading the room from the crack in the curtains, I had no desire to lift my head. Panic edged in when I did not recognize the room around me. Where were my clothes? I sat up, completely naked, and looked around. The dark-haired singer lying in the same bed smiled from his pillow.

I slid from the bed in search of my clothes and found them in the living room portion of his suite. I had no idea how I had gotten there. I did not remember anything after sipping the drink he sent to my table. I had no idea what we had done after arriving in his room. But he had certainly enjoyed it.

"Can we meet up in Reno next week?" he asked as I headed for the door.

I slammed the door behind me and stood in the hallway for a few minutes, shaking. I had barely enough time to shower in my own room and make it to the airport before my flight left.

On another trip to Denver, I sat at a small round table in a dimly lit lounge waiting for my dinner reservation. I swirled my glass of Chivas Regal, straight up. I liked its golden color and the way the lights danced over its surface. Its smooth woody fragrance brought my stress down several notches before the stout elixir even reached my tongue.

"May I join you?"

I turned to see the man to whom the deep voice belonged. Tall, with broad shoulders and a tan, square face, his blue-gray eyes looked directly into mine. His business suit spoke power, his smile spoke kindness. I was smitten immediately. The man of my dreams stood before me. I returned his easy smile and gestured towards the chair across from mine.

Conversation flowed easily. We enjoyed dinner together, then moved outside to the lounge chairs by the pool. Lights sparkled from underneath the water and fairy lights lit up the darkness around us. We spoke of our interests and hobbies. We spoke of places we had been and would like to go. We spoke of the easy chemistry between us and the future that had to be our destiny. The hours disappeared and suddenly it was midnight. We agreed to meet the next morning at that same restaurant at his hotel for breakfast before we each flew out the following afternoon to our own destinations: him to Portland, me to San Francisco. He spoke promises of a long-distance relationship. Our future was meant to be.

I floated in a dream back to my own hotel, alone. I slept the peaceful sleep of one happy and secure in life. The next morning, I packed my bags as butterflies danced in my stomach. I ached to see Robert and looked forward to breakfast with the man I hoped I would spend the rest of my life with. We hadn't even slept together, so this was a new adventure for me.

When I arrived at his hotel, I hurried to the restaurant. We had agreed to meet at 10:00 AM. The breakfast crowd was thinning out. I glanced in at the tables and didn't see him, so I sat in the lobby to await his arrival. The hand on my watch reached out for 10:30. I called his room, but there was no answer. At 10:45, my stomach sinking, I found his room, but the housekeeping staff was already cleaning the empty space. I checked at the front desk. He had checked out early that morning. The air left my lungs.

I made it to my car before the tears exploded. *Why?* I begged of an unknown god. *Why? He wasn't even trying to get me into bed. How could he be so wonderful, so caring, and then just disappear?* My heart shattered into a thousand pieces. Then the nausea came … overwhelming, but without response. I dreaded the flight home.

I drove to the airport in a daze. My stomach gnawed. My emotions left me empty. I couldn't feel any worse. How could a broken heart take me down so badly?

After I arrived home in Menlo Park, the sickness did not go away. In fact, two days later when it still pushed me down, I knew something was terribly wrong. I blamed Robert and my broken heart, but none of it made sense. I scheduled an appointment for the next day with my doctor.

After gathering all the facts and performing a cursory exam, she looked at me with a nearly blank face. "I'll give you three guesses at what's going on," she said, "And the last two don't count."

Completely ignorant as to what she was implying, I returned her blank stare.

"You're pregnant," she stated.

I sat, dumbfounded.

"What do you want to do about it?" she asked.

Again, I just stared.

She scheduled the abortion for the very next week.

ↄ ↄ ↄ ↄ ↄ

I was free once again. But what was freedom? Freedom was being able to pick up a stranger in a bar and have meaningless sex with him at home on my waterbed. Freedom was a stranger forcing amyl nitrate upon me during sex against my will. Freedom was picking up a lounge singer, then waking up the next morning, naked in his bed, with no idea how I got there, and no idea where my clothes might be. Freedom was getting pregnant by my boss and being able to get an abortion. Yes, I had my freedom again.

Sex is like drugs. You take a little to fill the emptiness but pretty soon that little bit doesn't do the job anymore. So, you take more and harder stuff and still, each time you come down, the emptiness remains. You reach a point of addiction from which there is no way out.

Perhaps it was a lack of love as a small child. Perhaps it was the things done to me by my stepfather. Perhaps I was just human, looking for all the same things for which everyone searches. For me, it was through sex that I searched for self-worth. If a man desired me, it gave me value. But no matter how many men I had, or how often I had them, or how perverted the sex might become, I had to keep coming back to that empty space that refused to be filled by the things that I chose.

I had everything every American girl dreams of. I was attractive. I had a glamorous job and a sexy sports car. I lived in a garden bungalow apartment and dated wealthy men and movie stars. But in November 1977, I wanted to end my life.

CR　CR　CR　CR　CR

I had everything every American girl dreams of ... but I wanted to end my life.

ଔ   ଔ   ଔ   ଔ   ଔ

18 – Light in the Darkness

"Darkness cannot drive out darkness: only light can do that."
Martin Luther King Jr.

In my Menlo Park bungalow, darkness hung in the air. A dim light from the stove reached for the man across the room. It revealed small glimpses of recognition. My real father. The father I could not grow up with. I didn't know him anymore. Darkness descended in my mind, trying to block even the flicker that occasionally danced off his glasses as he turned his head to look at me.

Why are you here now? I didn't want to face him. *If you would have been here thirteen years ago, perhaps it could have been different.* But he wasn't. The damage was done. *If you could have been here thirteen years ago, the night my stepfather first entered my bedroom, perhaps the years that followed might have been different.*

We had few words to exchange. I could not face the shame that confronted me in his presence, and he stumbled at attempts to break through the barrier I threw up. He slowly rose, mumbling about a morning conference. Relieved, I showed him to the door.

My father's visit could not have been more poorly timed. I was still reeling from a girlfriend's visit just moments earlier.

Her words had left me shaken. I was not ready to deal with any other intrusions.

"It's alright if you don't care what people know about you," she had self-righteously stated after our weekend with the Rugby team from Vancouver, British Columbia. "But because I hang around with you, it is ruining my reputation." The fact that Virginia behaved with as much promiscuity as me was not the issue. The issue was that those things were to be hidden in the daylight. I flaunted my behavior. That was who I was. I would not be hypocritical nor pretend otherwise. But her words slashed apart my final raiment of self-value.

The next morning, I stumbled through work, thankful that nobody needed any important information from me. At lunch, my new army-green MG roadster found its way home. My mind strayed behind me as I wandered through the door of my garden bungalow apartment. Then I sat, staring at nothing.

Struck by a sudden idea, I rifled through drawers until I found a pen and tablet. Emboldened with a plan, I needed to write it down. The thoughts flowed almost too quickly for the pen.

Christmas. I would do it on Christmas. Perhaps if I died then, somebody would notice, somebody might even care, or would they?

A gun. It had to be a gun. I needed to feel the pounding of the lead as it exploded in my brain. I read the words I was writing but there was no emotion attached. They were just words, and a plan. I no longer existed.

My thoughts blurred like a fog-shrouded sky. No ray of sunlight pierced the ominous shadows. No drop of rain fell from my dreary, dry eyes. I stared across the room at nothingness, at a room devoid of substance, like the space where my heart was supposed to reside.

Then, like an airplane emerging from the fog, the plant that stood in the corner of my living room took shape. The dieffenbachia. Leaf, by leaf, by leaf—large dark green leaves with yellow and cream-colored spatters dancing across each surface. They climbed the heavy stem nearly to the open beam ceiling. But there was something else. It tugged at my consciousness, begging me to focus.

A pit formed in my stomach as I began to recognize what I was seeing. I'd never seen them before. Flowers. Large, snow-white flowers, like jungle blossoms. Two of them. Each of them nearly eight inches across, peeling open like wide, split, banana skins, the golden yellow stamens reaching for the light. For a moment, I sat transfixed, as if there was nothing else in the world except me and those flowers; those flowers that had not been there before. In fact, that plant had never borne flowers. As far as I knew, dieffenbachias, aka Dumb Cane, did not bear flowers. Then, as the piercing of an arrow, I knew those flowers were a sign of hope from God.

My emotions exploded. Tears flowed like rivers down my cheeks, washing away all that was left of who I had been. My body shook with uncontrollable sobs as I reached out and felt the reality of God in my life.

The next morning the flowers were gone.

ଓ   ଓ   ଓ   ଓ   ଓ

Something had happened inside me. I could not deny it. But I didn't know what it was. There was a strange sense of peace deep inside. I knew God had something to do with it, but I wasn't quite ready to invite him into any more of my life than the little piece he occupied in the experience. The Bible said God was my father. I did not have a great track record with fathers.

I spent Thanksgiving with my brother and sister at a cabin in the mountains and quietly, stubbornly, muddled through it, finding only bits and pieces of half-hearted conversation. From then until Christmas I fell into a period of social hibernation. I didn't date or go out at all. I merely went to work each day and came home where I lingered over lonely dinners and mundane TV. Fortunately, there was no more travel for the month of December.

The new year arrived, and with it a desire to pick up the pieces and rebuild whatever it was I had lost during the last miserable seven years. Perhaps it was something I never had in the first place. Regardless of what it was, or may have been, I pursued it.

I pounded the racquetball until ready for competitions. I joined the Jack LaLanne European Health Spas, swimming, crunching, and steaming every night after work. I ran the track at a nearby high school, though my diminished heart performance from my rheumatic fever only allowed four times around, or one mile. I shed the extra twenty pounds gained during my extravagant living. As my health improved, so too did my attitude.

Easter morning, 1978, the sun peeked through the shades of my bedroom window. My emotions mirrored the dancing rays of sunlight reflecting off the pictures on my wall. I emerged from my self-imposed isolation. It was time to engage others in my life.

While the sun crept over the rooftops, I walked the two blocks to my sister Rhonda's house. She and her roommate were both Christians and, although I enjoyed their company, I resented the fact that they kept my name on a prayer list posted on their refrigerator. *They could have their religion, but they really should keep it to themselves.* But even that was not a damper on this particular morning.

Singing, laughing, and guitar music greeted me. A small group of people were enjoying Easter breakfast on their flower-shrouded patio. After several invitations to stay and join them, I found an empty chair on the edge of their circle. It wasn't long before I joined in the contagious singing, even though they were singing about a God I wasn't quite ready to embrace.

Late morning, they piled into their cars for a drive out to Half Moon Bay where their church held a large Easter baptismal service. Caught up in their celebration, I squeezed into one of the cars. There was always the chance I might stumble across a good-looking guy.

When we arrived at the beach, the baptisms were just finishing. We followed the small crowds of people back up to the pastor's weathered redwood house for fellowship, food, and drinks. I made my way through the clusters of chatting people, through the house and onto the aging wooden deck. There I saw Bob ... tall, tan, broad-shouldered, and blond. His screen-printed t-shirt quoted something about racquetball. I approached him with some line about the sport.

"Are you a Christian?" he asked.

Taken aback by the abruptness of his question, I responded, "Well, I believe that Jesus Christ died on the cross and rose again for our sins, but so what?" I had learned those words in Sunday school before I was seven years old, but they were just words, meaningless words. I didn't get it.

Bob spent the next several minutes trying to convince me that Jesus was indeed "the way, the truth, and the life." But I was far more interested in Bob's body than the Jesus he was trying to convince me of.

Seeing my lack of response, Bob finally said, "Follow me, there's somebody I want you to meet."

I tagged along behind him until we caught Leo on his way out the door. Leo was no knight in shining armor. Why Bob would stop him was beyond my wildest imaginations. He wasn't any taller than me and had a beer belly that hung out over his drooping greasy jeans, the offensive belly barely covered by his tattered, once-white T-shirt. His long, scraggly, black hair matched the beard on his face below his beady black eyes. His hesitant smile revealed black and rotting teeth.

"She wants to know why Jesus is important," Bob blurted.

Leo hesitated, frustration on his face. His eyes took me in then softened. Resignation echoed in his voice. "Come here, Sweetheart."

I obediently followed the scraggly-haired man to a window seat in the dining area where other people milled around in broken conversations. There Leo told me two very simple stories. I don't remember what those stories were, but the truth of the stories struck my heart with the bursting open of a gateway into a light such as I had never seen before. The truth was that "Jesus is God!" Suddenly it made all the difference in the world.

Other people in the room ceased their conversations, observing the transformation taking place on the window seat. At that moment, I opened my heart to Jesus Christ. He came in and touched me. Like a butterfly bursting from a cocoon, I broke free from my shame, emerged a new person.

I didn't know what happened. I just knew I felt different. Real love, like I had never known before, swelled within me and around me. I knew in my heart that Jesus had taken the sexual immorality away from me. I was washed clean.

My sister Rhonda had left earlier with friends, so was not witness to these events. In a separate car full of her friends, my journey back over the forested mountains played in a dream. Sunlight filtered through the towering canopy, dancing off every leaf and rock it touched. My mind danced with every sunbeam, free from the tethers of sin and darkness. Released from the chains of shame and guilt, a new emotion permeated my heart: hope.

As we climbed out of the car in front of Rhonda's house, Rhonda walked out to meet us. The moment she saw me, she knew. We froze, looking into each other's eyes, then ran and embraced. Laughing, I thanked her that my name had been written on her prayer list. And now I knew it was also written, *"... in the Lamb's book of life ..." (Revelation 13:8)*. And that meant eternal life with God.

All of this was new and a bit confusing to me, kind of like moving to a new house in a new town. But I eagerly set out to explore. God's love overwhelmed me, and I happily loved Him back. I wanted to please Him like a child seeks to please a parent. I had never known that kind of relationship from my birth parents. I held out my hand for Him to take and guide me through the challenges each day, and He did just that. I woke up every morning and recognized joy and hope. This was uncharted territory, but I knew I would never be alone again.

ରୁ ରୁ ରୁ ରୁ ରୁ

I was tested in my newfound faith just a few short weeks later. Carl, one of the buyers at my company, a married man with whom I had been intimate, was coming out from New York. We had planned to meet in Las Vegas for a few days before he made his way to our offices on the West Coast. When he called to finalize the plans, I told him I couldn't go.

"Why not?" he demanded, his agitation traversing the phone line.

"I'll talk to you when you get here," was all I could reply. It wasn't the sort of thing I could explain over the phone, especially when I didn't understand it myself.

Lament besieged me. Rejoicing did not follow my act of faith. I really did want to meet Carl in Las Vegas.

"Okay God! What's the deal?" I challenged. "I acted on faith and now I feel like crap. Where's the joy I'm supposed to feel in following you?"

I called Leo. The man who led me to Jesus Christ had become my spiritual mentor. I met him at my sister's house where he shared passages from the Bible with me and assured me I had done the right thing. My frustration remained. I straggled home defeated.

Lying in bed that night, I continued mulling things over, challenging God on this faith issue. I picked up my Bible, brown leather with my name engraved on it, given to me by my sister and her friends shortly after Easter. But I didn't have a clue how to use it. I just opened the book and stared at the page in front of me. There, on that page, I read:

"And without faith it is impossible to please God, because anyone who comes to him must believe that he exists and that he rewards those who earnestly seek him." (Hebrews 11:6)

I breathed in the deep rest of a peaceful night, secure in the knowledge that God really did care about me.

Shortly after severing my personal ties with Carl, Georges called from the Club Med, Playa Blanca, Mexico. I had danced many a starlit night on the beach while he played the trombone, part of the Club Med band. We had become very close during my recent two-week vacation there; he even nursed me through a devastating bout of "you-know-what-happens-when-you-drink-the-water-in-Mexico."

"Charcoal works really well," he indicated in broken English. Georges, from Switzerland, spoke French, yet we somehow managed to communicate in tender love languages.

Through a translator, Georges let me know when I could pick him up at the San Francisco airport for a week's stay before his transfer to a Caribbean Club Med location. My life, my morals, my being had been entirely transformed since my last night with Georges. I enjoyed Georges. I cared for Georges. I needed to tell him about God in my life. I needed to tell him the truth about Jesus Christ and why it mattered. I had no idea where to begin. The language barrier, of course, presented a major hurdle.

It was at Pastor Ron Richie's house in Half Moon Bay that I met Jesus Christ, Ron Richie of Peninsula Bible Church, then in Palo Alto. I reached out to him and his wife, Anne Marie Richie, a lovely and wonderful French gal. In a sun-drenched living room, as I watched from the sofa, she shared with Georges the truths I had just stumbled into, truths I didn't know how to live, but truths I wanted to know more about and share with him.

It would be months later when Georges would call me from the Caribbean to tell me a fellow band member was a Christian. In his broken English, he told me, "Now two people have told me about The Way."

His life had changed as my life had changed, and mine had changed dramatically in those months following Easter. I no longer dated but found myself in the company of a group of people my own age who shared regular Bible studies together. We did a lot of other things together as well: dinners out, potlucks, movies, swim parties, Disneyland, dancing.

Since I no longer needed the privacy of my own place for "dates," I welcomed a roommate. About a week after Bonnie moved in, I received a call from Ken, a stockbroker I met while on that now-infamous Club Med vacation. Ken was not a Christian and I knew I was playing with fire when I accepted his offer of dinner and an evening together. Bonnie encouraged me to "go for it."

As time drew near for my date with Ken, I longed for some of the physical feelings in a relationship with a man. I prayed in my car on the way to the city, "Lord, I really want to get laid tonight. So, if you don't want me to, then you're going to have to do something about it!" I felt sacrilegious in my prayer, but it was truth.

That evening over dinner I was appalled to hear myself telling Ken about Jesus. He kept changing the subject. After dinner, back at Ken's place, we undressed and settled into the hot tub. He slid next to me, touching me. Enticing as it was, a new sense of strength swept over me. I stood up and stepped out of the hot tub.

"Wait. What?" Ken sputtered.

"Sorry, I gotta go." I waved without looking back. I put on my clothes, strode to my car, and drove off. Driving home on the freeway I sang, shouted, and laughed like an idiot.

"Yay, God! You did it!"

ᘓ   ᘓ   ᘓ   ᘓ   ᘓ

Spring passed into summer. Bonnie and I moved into a large three-bedroom apartment in Sunnyvale, with another friend of ours, Debbie. I had never experienced so much peace or enjoyed the people and things around me so much.

People at work saw the changes in me and often asked what happened. "It's God," I said, then smiled and pointed up. God amazed me at all the little miracles He accomplished, simply at the request of my prayers. It wasn't long before one of my associates asked me to pray for her brother who had just been diagnosed with a serious illness. How was I supposed to pray for something that big? I didn't know, but I did talk to God about it. I just talked to him like I would talk to another person. Somebody told me that was praying. I don't know if her brother was healed or not, but she was greatly comforted. And, somehow I knew God heard my prayers. In the Bible it states: *This is the confidence we have in approaching God: that if we ask anything according to his will, he hears us." (I John 5:14)* And I knew that!

My roommates and I attended our church picnic in early September. I was in charge of some of the games and noticed a new face that kept coming through my line. Flattered at the attention from a good-looking guy, I finally smiled and met his eyes. He spoke with a European accent.

"From Poland," he said, and asked me to join him for dinner.

Dinner, wine, and his charm stirred reminiscent passions. For the first time in months, I found myself in another man's bed. I felt I had let God down, and that was not a direction I wanted to go. The next morning, I met Alek at church.

"I can't go out with you anymore," I explained without regret. "You are interfering in my walk with God." I knew that walk with God was far more important than any man. Alek didn't respond, nor did I ever see him at church again.

Convinced I had done the right thing, and certain that God would take care of my felt need for a man, I handed that part of my life over to Him. I wanted to do it His way. I had already proven my way led to dead ends and darkness. God had shown me a light in my darkness, a light that revealed true and honest love, a light worth pursuing.

Jesus said, "... *I am the light of the world. Whoever follows me will never walk in darkness, but will have the light of life.*" *(John 8:12)*

ଓ ଓ ଓ ଓ ଓ

19 – Worthy of Love

*"God loves you even in your darkest hours. He comforts you even
in your darkest moments. He forgives you even
in your darkest failures."*
Unknown

Later that same day, September 10, one of my new
friends, Laura, invited me to her birthday party, a potluck
barbecue in a well-to-do neighborhood of Hillsdale. On the way,
I stopped and bought a nice steak and dessert. Most of the guests
had already arrived by the time I got there. Laughing, chatting
people mingled both inside and out of the large house. I stopped
by the kitchen, gave Laura a hug, and deposited my
contributions to the afternoon fare. Delighted to see Leo, I ran
over and hugged him. Leo introduced me to a friend of his I had
not yet met. His friend was putting the final touches on a green
salad.

"This," Leo gestured towards the nondescript
bespectacled man, "is my very best friend and brother in the
Lord."

"Hi," I offered, and then casually picked up the salad
tongs and began to stir his handiwork.

He snatched the tongs out of my hands.

"I just arranged those layers," he muttered as he laid the tongs out of my reach and rearranged the cucumber slices I had just displaced.

Startled at his response, and unaware he had been perfecting what he apparently considered to be the perfect salad, I excused myself and realized, without regret, I didn't even get his name. I flitted from group to group, enjoying the sun and the people.

As fate would have it, when I sat down to enjoy my steak, I was seated next to "Salad Man," aka Thomas. Thomas and Leo were supposed to be over in the Sierras that weekend where they had a ministry to teenage kids at a youth camp. One odd event after another had prevented them from actually leaving the Bay Area. Convinced that maybe God was trying to tell them something, Leo suggested Laura's birthday party instead. Thomas had met her once before and, although he really didn't appreciate such gatherings, he was glad to come, only because it was Laura.

His manner was now much more amenable, though without apology. By the time our steaks were half-eaten, our conversation had evolved into intense discussion about the moral realities of our lives. We agreed on a number of topics and I found myself disclosing things to him I hadn't even shared with some of my closest friends.

With the last bite of steak, Tom abruptly interjected, "Well, if we're going to go for that bike ride, we better get going."

"Excuse me?" My mind lagged somewhere between the last complete sentence and the last bite of steak.

He continued in the tone of an instructor delivering a very dry lesson in chemistry. "I don't usually give girls rides."

So why are you giving me a ride? And on what bike? My mind sputtered in confusion but the words couldn't find their way out.

He rose solemnly from the bench, turned and headed for the house, without looking back to even see if I was following. Without another word he strode through the house and out the front door. Despite my bewilderment, I scurried behind him.

The "bike" was a chopped Harley Roadster with a teal-colored gas tank. A flash of sunlight off the chrome sissy bar momentarily blinded me. I didn't see his outstretched arm dangling the glittery blue motorcycle helmet in my direction.

"Here." He jabbed it at me. "You need to wear this. Not that I mind," he added, "but the government seems to think it has the right to tell me how I'm going to ride my bike."

I took the helmet from his hand, fitted it on my head, and flashed a smile. But his back was already turned. He put on his own helmet. I climbed onto the back of the bike, found the foot pegs for my feet, and leaned back into the sissy bar.

The motorcycle ride took us on the breathtaking Junipero Serra freeway, a gently flowing river of concrete that stole intentionally across the ridge that separated the peninsula cities from the Pacific Ocean. The abundant lush greenery of the mountainsides bordered the then quiet freeway on that still September evening. The sun was setting low in the sky and the wind on my face felt delicious. I laughed inside about the jokes made of happy bikers:

"How can you recognize a happy biker?"

"By the bugs in his teeth."

I leaned closer into Thomas to keep from eating the bugs myself.

The stillness and beauty of the evening was broken only by the intrusion of the Harley's engine. My motorcycle helmet, like a glittery blue cocoon, wrapped itself around my senses until the roar of the engine dissipated into a distant past. My mind wandered through the windswept cypress and the giant redwoods. I imagined what it must have been like to be among the early Spanish explorers; with those who breached these verdant peaks for the very first time and gazed upon the haunting beauty of San Francisco Bay, unobstructed by asphalt jungles, before man's upheaval disrupted its pristine silence.

The rumble of a passing semi yanked me from the mountaintop and back to reality. I wrapped my arms tighter around Tom but resisted pressing my face into his shoulder.

If this man asked me to marry him tonight, I would say yes.

I shook my head, stunned at the words burrowing their way through my mind. *Where did that come from?* I glanced at the back of his helmet and studied his broad shoulders. *I don't even know you. I don't even know where you live.* My thoughts bristled but my potential fiancé seemed oblivious to my argument, until the motorcycle slowed abruptly, and Tom eased onto the dusty shoulder.

For a brief moment, I panicked. *Surely he can't read my mind, can he?*

He brought the bike to a halt, pushed down the kickstand and stood up. I let go of him and let my left foot drop to the pavement. He didn't turn around, but just stood there for a moment.

What if he brought me up here to kill me? In a split second my mind raced through a murder scenario. *Please, God, let a highway patrolman come by now.* I nearly hyperventilated.

"Gas cap fell off," he mumbled as he climbed off the bike.

"Oh." My thoughts relaxed but my breathing and heart rate were still on the fast track. I slipped off the back of the bike and shoved my hands into my jeans' pockets.

Tom walked back over the route we had just traveled. I humbly felt a responsibility to help and followed him a short distance down the road. At that point, we separated in different directions scouring the roadside grass.

As I searched for the gas cap, I stole an occasional glance at Tom. He wasn't really bad looking after all. His rugged yet angular face bore a remarkable resemblance to the actor Clint Eastwood. The aberrant thought that sneaked into my mind, just before the flight of the gas cap, had not gone away. *Why in the world would this man suddenly become a marriage prospect? Was I really that desperate?* I pushed the idea back in my mind when I spotted the cap in the grass across a ditch.

"I found it," I called out and waved it above my head.

We reached the bike at the same time and Tom replaced the cap without a word—not even a word of thanks. He handed me my helmet.

"We better head back," he said without looking at me. He waited for me to climb on the back and then strapped on his own helmet. That was the extent of our conversation. He turned around at the next exit and we made our way back to the party. Nobody even realized we had been gone.

When I arrived home that evening, I called my sister, Rhonda. "I've met the man I'm going to marry," I told her without any real excitement.

Dead silence on the other end of the line.

"Are you there?"

Rhonda laughed and sputtered, "You met this guy tonight and now you want to marry him?"

"I didn't say that. I said he's the man I'm going to marry."

"And you know this because?"

"I just know it."

"And God told you this?"

"Well, yeah."

She proceeded to throw everything at me I had already thought of: I knew nothing about him; I didn't particularly like him; I had no idea who he was except that he was a friend of Leo's. Of course, with Leo as his only reference, she wasn't duly impressed. Leo's appearance was something of a thorn-in-the-flesh to some more conservative social Christians. Rhonda was not hypocritical. She just didn't know him very well at that point. I didn't have answers to any of those questions, but I knew I would marry this man.

"God, if this is you," I prayed that week, "I'm going to keep my hands out of it." I went so far as to look up his phone number in the telephone book for a town I had never even heard of. But I refused to call him. No, if this was God, then God would bring it about. I had learned that my choices only led me into disasters.

When the phone rang early the following Saturday morning, I groaned and turned my head on the pillow. I fumbled with the receiver and banged it against my ear.

"Yes?" Spit dribbled down my chin.

"I don't know if you remember me ..." he started.

I nearly choked and bolted upright in bed. I wiped the slobber from my face. It was Tom. I sat speechless. He explained that Leo was there for the weekend and wondered if I might want to come down and join them.

"I ... I ... I'd love to!" I stammered.

He then asked if I could stop on my way down and pick up a young man he had hired. Tom was vice president of a mining operation a couple of hours south of the Bay Area in the

Coast Range. It never even occurred to me that maybe his primary reason for inviting me down was to give this young man a ride. I grabbed some essentials and flew out the door. My roommates screamed out after me that I was crazy. I knew that, but nothing was going to keep me from this adventure.

ભ   ભ   ભ   ભ   ભ

The late October sun drenched the golden California hills with the warmth of an Indian Summer. Small twisted scrub oaks and red-barked manzanita trees staked multiple claims throughout the small canyon, with scattered Digger Pines standing sentry. The remnant of a stream gasped its last gurgles through the nearby rocky creek bed, hungry for a new season of rain. The uneven ground in the grassy clearing pushed gently through the wool blanket I lay on in my blue denim jeans, next to my sleeping husband.

Three days after we were married, Tom and I had hiked up the small canyon about a quarter mile to the spring that supplied our household water, making sure there was adequate depth for the placement of the black plastic PVC pipes that carried the water to the large redwood tanks on the hill above our little one-room cabin. For drinking water, Tom made weekly trips to town with four or five plastic five-gallon bakery buckets, wiped with vinegar, then filled with the town of Coalinga's tap water. An old-fashioned large aluminum ladle hung from a kitchen drawer, above the closed bucket, to dip drinks.

Tom managed a small mining operation in the Coast Range, about an hour west of Coalinga, in Los Gatos Canyon. Our small 400-square-foot cabin had originally been built as a lab for an earlier operation. Now, mining timbers created a sleeping loft strong enough to hold my waterbed. Our nearest neighbors, besides coyotes and rattlesnakes, lived eight miles away.

Tom's father, and subsequently Tom, owned "grand-daddy" claims on the 198 acres surrounding the Archer Mine, a cinnabar mine, or mercury ore. We were five miles out a dirt road behind two locked gates and surrounded by thousands of acres of federal BLM property. A nearby cattle ranch owned a portion between the Archer Mine and the main road, so our drive home often involved waiting on cattle crossings. Although we did have telephone service in our remote location, the electric lines did not reach to our little part of the world. I had left civilization cold turkey … and I reveled in the newness of living in the "sticks."

This particular day, we packed a picnic lunch of crusty French bread, cheeses, fruits, and wine, the detritus now scattered around us while the afternoon bade us remain under its brilliant blue skies. Full stomachs plus the warmth of the day lulled Tom to sleep. I basked in the stillness, smells, and beauty of nature surrounding me.

Peace, beyond what I had ever experienced, permeated to my core. I had willingly and eagerly left my busy, materialistic career world behind. And with it, everything of who I had been. I had no deadlines, no pressures, no expectations … nothing except to embrace the love around me. First, love from a God who pursued me through the muddiest of gutters, saved me from death at my own hand, and then welcomed me with joy. At that single moment when I asked Him to be in my life, to take my heart in His hands, He pushed my darkness away. The Bible says He took my sins and threw them as far as the east is from the west.

"For as high as the heavens are above the earth, so great is his love for those who fear him; as far as the east is from the west, so far has he removed our transgressions from us." (Psalms 103:11-12)

I was washed clean by the blood that Jesus Christ shed on the cross ... for me!

"... Though your sins are like scarlet, they shall be as white as snow; though they are red as crimson, they shall be like wool." (Isaiah 1:18)

I had lived in my own guilt and shame for so long, I believed I didn't deserve anything but death. I lived a life on the outside that invoked jealousy from others but, inside, hopelessness clawed like the constant sting of a scorpion. I had been ready to end it. There was no point in going any further. Sportscars, glamorous jobs, wealthy men ... none of it filled that hole in my heart that only God could fill. He filled that hole and, at the same time, lifted the weight of the burdens completely off of me. He removed the sting of death, replaced the empty hopelessness with hope itself. Like the butterfly completely shed of its cocoon, my wings were free, reflecting a kaleidoscope of color on my life and my emotions.

I looked at the sleeping man next to me. He loved me. The morning after our wedding night, I woke up actually feeling like a different person. My life was joined to his life. We were in this together. I was not so naïve to believe that everything from thereon would be a bed of roses. I just had a new foundation to stand on. But it took me letting God build that foundation.

The sun slipped behind the hills and coolness slithered through the canyon. Tom woke up, smiled, and pulled me close. After a tender kiss, we gathered up our things and headed back out to the dirt road. In the gathering darkness of our cabin, he lit a kerosene lamp. The flame danced. It glowed through the crystal-clear chimney filling the cabin with its soft light. The adventure of the rest of my life lay open before me, bathed in God's light.

My life was radically changed from darkness to light, from hopelessness to joy, from abuse to empowerment, by one simple truth: the truth of God's love, the truth of Jesus Christ's sacrifice on the cross for me ... and for you. Does that mean there are no more troubles in my life? No. It means that God is going through those troubles with me because of his overwhelming, never-ending, unconditional, and amazing love for me. And it is available to you:

"For God so loved the world that he gave his one and only Son, that whoever believes in him shall not perish but have eternal life." (John 3:16)

"Look at the birds of the air; they do not sow or reap or store away in barns, and yet your heavenly Father feeds them. Are you not much more valuable than they?" (Matthew 6:26)

This is not "The End" ... *it is my beginning!*

ଓ   ଓ   ଓ   ଓ   ଓ

Psalm 103
"Praise the LORD, my soul; all my inmost being,
praise his holy name.
Praise the LORD, my soul, and forget not all his benefits—who
forgives all your sins and heals all your diseases, who redeems
your life from the pit and crowns you with love and compassion,

who satisfies your desires with good things so that your youth is
renewed like the eagle's.
The LORD *works righteousness and justice for all the oppressed.*
He made known his ways to Moses, his deeds to the people of
Israel: The LORD *is compassionate and gracious, slow to anger,*
abounding in love.
He will not always accuse, nor will he harbor his anger
forever; he does not treat us as our sins deserve or repay us
according to our iniquities.
For as high as the heavens are above the earth, so great is his
love for those who fear him; as far as the east is from the west,
so far has he removed our transgressions from us.
As a father has compassion on his children, so the LORD *has*
compassion on those who fear him; for he knows how we are
formed, he remembers that we are dust.
The life of mortals is like grass, they flourish like a flower of the
field; the wind blows over it and it is gone,
and its place remembers it no more.
But from everlasting to everlasting the LORD's *love is with those*
who fear him, and his righteousness with their children's
children— with those who keep his covenant and remember to
obey his precepts.
The LORD *has established his throne in heaven,*
and his kingdom rules over all.
Praise the LORD, *you his angels, you mighty ones who do his*
bidding, who obey his word.
Praise the LORD, *all his heavenly hosts,*
you his servants who do his will.
Praise the LORD, *all his works everywhere in his dominion.*
Praise the LORD, *my soul."*

ଔ   ଔ   ଔ   ଔ   ଔ

Look for other titles by Deborah Silva:
Available in Fall/Winter 2020

Billy Goats, Rattlesnakes, and Jesus

A memoir of escape from the predator of spousal abuse in the name of God.

Billy Goats, Rattlesnakes, and Jesus is a true-story journey through spousal abuse and discovering what the Bible really has to say about it. Set against a very unique backdrop, it is also a story of God's modern-day miracles and love.

In 1978, Deborah, a brand-new Christian, leaves her glamorous career in the fashion industry and plunges into a life with her new husband, Tom. Living in a remote one-room cabin with no electricity, she must learn new skills like splitting wood and shooting rattlesnakes for dinner. Along with the physical challenges of her new environment, she comes face to face with contradictions between Biblical truth and Tom's imposed interpretation of truth, enclosing her in a false prison of submission.

Tom grows to believe he is the only one who has true understanding from God. He sees his responsibility before God to shape his family into perfection, whatever that takes, including isolation and brute force. Trapped by narrow interpretations of scriptures, Deborah struggles to find freedom for herself and her three daughters, all of whom were born at home with no midwife, and no government-registered birth certificates. Through the darkness, she is surprised by a living God who overwhelms with love and freedom.

more titles:

Off Ramp: God's Exit from Abuse
A journey of Hope and awakening to Biblical Answers about abuse.

Off Ramp, God's Exit from Abuse offers hope not only to victims of domestic violence and survivors of child abuse, but especially to Christian abuse victims who feel trapped by the confines of narrowly interpreted scriptures. Sadly, one in four women in the church is or has been a victim of abuse.

For the victim blinded by oppression, it is difficult to see the road signs pointing the way to the off ramp of safety, hope, and recovery. For the observer wanting to intervene, it is difficult to understand why the victim can't see the road signs. It is the role of the church to guide the victim to the safety of the off ramp, and to the Savior who offers hope, peace, and joy. Off Ramp provides answers and prescribes actions.

Written through memoir, counseling, and ministry, Off Ramp is intended first to the victim or potential victim, then secondly to those wishing to help, both as individuals and as a church. My own story travels through repeated child sexual abuse, to self-abuse even amidst worldly success as prom queen, beauty pageant queen, and Playboy centerfold model, to spousal abuse as a "baby Christian" in an isolated location with a man who felt he was the only one who had true understanding from God.

With God's miraculous provision, I escaped with my three daughters, all born at home and needing court-ordered birth certificates, to a life filled with the blessings and peace of a loving Savior. We broke the cycles of abuse.

Mastering the Art of Honey-n-Whole Wheat Cooking
(Printed replica of the book described in *Billy Goats, Rattlesnakes, and Jesus.*)
Available Winter 2020/Spring 2021

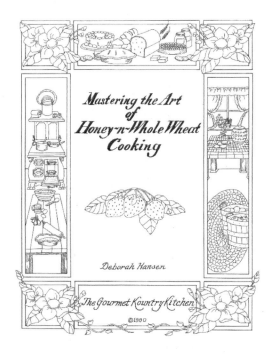

Original recipes and how-to tutorials developed in the little one-room cabin at the Archer Mine. Includes award-winning recipes and original artwork.

Written in the days before gluten was an issue (though most recipes work well substituting gluten-free flours for whole wheat), *Mastering the Art ...* covers everything from breakfast goodies, cakes, cookies, pies, and award-winning cheesecakes to canning, soups, salads, main dishes, and "A Hassle-Free Thanksgiving Dinner." All recipes are made using whole wheat flour, honey (in place of sugar)—oh, and lots of real butter.

ℭ   ℭ   ℭ   ℭ   ℭ